From Survive to Thrive
A Director's Guide for Leading an Early Childhood Program

Debbie LeeKeenan and Iris Chin Ponte

D1319444

National Association for the Education of Young Children

Washington, DC

National Association for the
Education of Young Children
1401 H Street NW, Suite 600
Washington, DC 20005
202-232-8777 • 800-424-2460
NAEYC.org

NAEYC Books

Senior Director, Publishing and
Professional Learning
Susan Friedman

Editor in Chief
Kathy Charner

Senior Creative Design Manager
Audra Meckstroth

Senior Editor
Holly Bohart

Publishing Manager
Francine Markowitz

Creative Design Specialist
Charity Coleman

Associate Editor
Rossella Procopio

Through its publications
program, the National
Association for the Education
of Young Children (NAEYC)
provides a forum for discussion
of major issues and ideas in the
early childhood field, with the
hope of provoking thought and
promoting professional growth.
The views expressed or implied
in this book are not necessarily
those of the Association.

Permissions

NAEYC accepts requests for limited use of
our copyrighted material. For permission
to reprint, adapt, translate, or otherwise
reuse and repurpose content from this
publication, review our guidelines at
NAEYC.org/resources/permissions.

The figure on page 3 is adapted from
P.J. Bloom, *Leadership in Action: How
Effective Leaders Get Things Done* 2nd ed.
(Lake Forest, IL: New Horizons, 2014), 4.

The figure "Some Similarities in Guiding
Children and Guiding Adults" on page
7 is reprinted, with permission, from G.
Schweikert, *Being a Supervisor: Winning
Ways for Early Childhood Professionals* (St.
Paul, MN: Redleaf Press, 2014), 19.

Photo Credits

Copyright © NAEYC: 75 and 92
Copyright © Erin Donn: 71
Copyright © Bob Ebbesen: 66
Copyright © Julia Luckenbill: 61 and 107
Copyright © Syretha Storey: 41 and 68
Copyright © Lakshini Wijeweera: 29
Copyright © Getty Images: 9, 10, 18, 22,
24, 54, 58, 62 (all), 99, 104, 123, 128, 141,
145, 153, and 161
Courtesy of the authors: 83 and 90
Courtesy of Hilltop Children's Center: 115

**From Survive to Thrive: A Director's
Guide for Leading an Early Childhood
Program.** Copyright © 2018 by the
National Association for the Education
of Young Children. All rights reserved.
Printed in the United States of America.

Library of Congress Control Number:
2018935989

ISBN: 978-1-938113-36-9

Item 1136

Contents

Preface

In recent years, directing an early childhood program has become more complicated due to increasing regulatory and licensing demands, accountability pressures, an expanding knowledge base in the field, and the changing diversity and demographics of programs. Program directors are busier than ever with multiple demands on their limited time. While there are excellent books on reflective leadership and on program administration and management (see References on pages 162–165 and additional resources listed in the "Go Deeper" sidebars at the end of each chapter), the focus of this book is the integration of theory and practice of leading early childhood programs, including outlining effective strategies that program directors can use immediately.

We authors are program leaders at different points in our professional paths. Debbie has more than 45 years of experience teaching and directing, including directing the Eliot-Pearson Children's School, the laboratory school affiliated with the Eliot-Pearson Department of Child Study and Human Development at Tufts University, from 1996 to 2013. Iris leads her own early childhood program in her home, the Henry Frost Children's Program, which she established in 2010. Our combined perspectives and experiences in the field as a veteran leader and an emerging leader have shaped and informed this book.

We also had the privilege of interviewing and meeting with program directors from around the country for this book. Their insights on the rewards and challenges of being directors are included in quotes and anecdotes throughout these pages. While their programs represent diverse early childhood education settings—serving low- and high-income populations, located in rural and urban communities, and operating as large corporate and small family-run centers—these directors all have a common passion and dedication to children and families.

This book is a resource for directors and administrators of early childhood programs serving children from birth to age 5. The topics, frameworks, and strategies covered create a foundation for those new to the role, but directors at all levels of experience and serving in a variety of settings will find the information useful. Many of the ideas in this book were first introduced in *Leading Anti-Bias Early Childhood Programs: A Guide for Change*, which Debbie coauthored with Louise Derman-Sparks and John Nimmo. That book focuses on the concepts of leadership in the context of anti-bias change, and we have applied many of the same ideas more broadly to the role of the program director here. Our goal is to provide a rationale for best practices of leadership and, at the same time, offer practical tips and strategies you can implement in your program. We hope this book will not only support your growth as a current or aspiring program director but also serve as a resource you return to whenever you are looking for a new idea or solution.

Chapter One

What Does It Mean to Be a Director?

Leadership is the capacity to translate vision into reality.

—**Warren G. Bennis,** *Executive's Portfolio of Model Speeches for All Occasions*

Terms Used in this Book

There are many titles used in early childhood programs nationwide for education administrators. Throughout this book, *director* and *program leader* are used interchangeably to be inclusive of all programs, both large and small.

Directors have a diverse set of responsibilities, and managing them all can often feel like a delicate balancing act. You have to provide a safe, healthy environment for children and teachers. Hire and retain a qualified, diverse staff. Have a solid business plan. Understand child development and best practices in early childhood education. Establish collaborative relationships with families and program stakeholders. Market your program. Help out in a classroom when you're needed. Take time to care for your own physical and emotional health. Remain calm under pressure.

Your overall responsibility is to create a physically and emotionally safe educational environment where learning and care can flourish for children, staff, and families. To do this, you must prioritize your duties and tasks on an ongoing basis and focus on what is most important at any particular moment, even as you keep an eye on the long term.

The Director as Both Manager and Leader

Many writers have noted the differences between the role of a manager and that of a leader (see Carter & Curtis 2010; Talan & Bloom 2011). A manager focuses on people, problems, and tasks. A leader must tend to these managerial functions while bringing them into focus with the program's shared vision, mission, and goals (see pages 28–31 in Chapter 3 for information on developing these important elements of your program). Effective program directors are both leaders *and* managers. As directors develop professionally, their acquisition of skills follows a predictable progression. In the beginning, it is common to focus on your managerial functions out of necessity—the immediate daily tasks that are the nuts and bolts of running a program. As you put processes in place and develop confidence and self-efficacy, you gradually widen your focus to include the big picture—long-range vision building and systemic changes. The figure on the next page, based in part on Bloom's (2014) distinctions between the functions of management and leadership, illustrates elements of both of these sides of early childhood administration.

Managers...

> Focus on efficiency
> Value stability
> Concentrate on organizing systems
> Focus on short-term goals
> Establish work plans

Directors...

> Focus on efficiency *and* effectiveness
> Value stability *and* risk taking
> Concentrate on organizing systems *and* motivating people
> Focus on short- *and* long-term goals
> Establish work plans *and* co-establish the vision and mission

Leaders...

> Focus on effectiveness
> Value risk taking
> Concentrate on motivating people
> Focus on long-term goals
> Co-establish the vision and mission

Adapted from P.J. Bloom, *Leadership in Action: How Effective Leaders Get Things Done*, 2nd ed.

Know Yourself

Developing your leadership skills is a journey, and it begins with some self-examination.

Recognizing Your Personal Attributes

Understanding your strengths, weaknesses, emotions, and motivations is an important part of being a leader. Self-awareness of your skills enables you to identify which ones contribute to the effectiveness of the program and which you need to hone. A director rarely has all the skills needed to lead a program. While building on your strengths, look for ways to further develop your abilities to communicate, forge relationships, make sound financial decisions, or whatever other skills you need.

Reflecting on your beliefs and motivations provides insight into your emotions, another essential ingredient for effective leadership. Consider your blind spots, such as a tendency to refuse to ask for or accept help, a reluctance to take a stand on unpopular issues, or being unwilling to confront individuals when necessary. How do these affect your interactions with others and your ability to get things done? When engaging with a staff member or family with whom you disagree, it is easy for your emotions to cloud the situation. When this occurs, take a few moments to reflect on why you might be experiencing a particular emotion, like this director:

> During the second week of school, Midori is approached by a teacher, Jo, in the program she directs. Jo tells Midori about a situation she believes is a parent–child separation issue in her classroom. Each morning when 3-year-old Zelda Maisel arrives with her mother, Mrs. Maisel insists on spoon-feeding Zelda her breakfast at the snack table. She is upset that Mrs. Maisel does not let her child feed herself, something Jo has been working on with Zelda at lunch and snack time, and asks Midori to intervene.
>
> Midori's first reaction is that Jo is in the right and Zelda must be allowed to feed herself. Not only is it program policy, but Midori firmly believes that it is also a necessary part of developing self-care and fine motor skills. She feels that it is difficult for some parents to give their young children opportunities to develop independence and thinks that perhaps Zelda's mother is pampering her daughter. However, before responding to Jo, Midori takes a moment to consider Zelda's family's culture and background. A few interactions Midori personally had with Mrs. Maisel suggested that she does not tolerate waste. It might be that she feeds Zelda to avoid having food spilled and wasted. Midori mentions this to Jo. Together, they discuss why the situation is challenging and what they could do to support both Jo's goals for children in the classroom and the family's goals that center on feeding and eating.

When you are able to recognize and separate your emotions from a situation, you are calmer and can consider a variety of perspectives. This allows you to address the situation in a collaborative, productive way.

Identifying Your Leadership Traits

In addition to your skills and emotional makeup, your personal values and beliefs influence your day-to-day leading of the program as well as your organization's overall purpose and goals. When you integrate your personal principles and professional voice, you will find the strength, passion, and—most important—the authority to lead others (Espinosa 1997). One way to start identifying your own values and beliefs is by thinking about leaders and mentors in your life who have inspired or disappointed you. What qualities and traits have you admired most in other leaders? What qualities have you disliked?

Here are some questions to help you think about your own leadership traits and your approach to professional relationships:

> Am I organized and good with details or more of a big-picture person?

> Do I tend to be outgoing or more reserved?

> Do I work collaboratively, or do I use a more authoritative approach with others? In what situations am I more likely to act in each way? Why?

> When faced with a task, do I focus more on getting the task done or on the best way to do so? How does it vary with the situation?

> How comfortable am I with disequilibrium and conflict? How do I tend to handle situations involving them?

> How flexible am I?

> Is my communication style more direct or indirect?

> Do I make decisions easily and quickly, or do I take my time?

> Do I keep my feelings to myself or freely show them?

> Do I stick with methods I know work, or do I tend to consider more unique approaches?

Consider how these qualities affect your relationships with staff, families, and children.

Practice Facilitative Leadership

Your leadership traits strongly influence how you work with your staff, the families, and others involved in the program. While many types of leadership styles have been identified, we advocate *facilitative leadership*, a process where the power and responsibility to meet an organization's goals are shared (Forester 2013). This means finding ways to create partnerships with staff and give them a greater voice on issues that affect them every day, such as resource allocation, curriculum, and scheduling. Facilitative leadership also means constructing meaningful relationships with families by providing them with opportunities to weigh in on parent policies and their children's daily experiences. Facilitative leaders invite and inspire group participation, proactively involving staff and families to contribute ideas and perspectives about improving center processes. Facilitative leaders build on individuals' strengths, increase engagement, and help others learn how to learn (O'Neill & Brinkerhoff 2018). That said, there are decisions that ultimately are the director's responsibility, such as hiring staff or budgetary issues. Even in those situations, an effective leader gathers input from staff and families before making a final decision. Regardless of a tendency to lead in a certain way, an effective director adapts to each situation as needed.

Treat Teachers the Same Way You Expect Teachers to Treat Children

Many of the most effective program directors started as classroom teachers, and there are a number of parallels between working with children and working with adults that can help you in your director role. A teacher's job is to create a classroom community where children feel safe to independently learn, problem solve, and take risks, and a director needs to create the same type of space for the teachers in her program. Just as teachers see each child as an individual with unique strengths and challenges, directors should recognize the same in each teacher. Deep learning occurs for both children and adults when they have opportunities to try new things, can make mistakes that they can learn from, and are supported by others who have more understanding or skill. At any age, we all feel more motivated and invested in our learning when our voices are included in the process, whether that means letting a child choose which center to visit first that day or giving teachers the flexibility to choose materials for their classroom.

Setting goals and objectives for learning is another parallel process. Teachers observe children, discover what they already know and can do, and scaffold learning experiences to help children develop their knowledge and skills. Effective directors—whether they are developing or mature leaders—not only supervise their staff but also mentor them and help them set professional development goals (see pages 112–116 in Chapter 7). And directors as well as teachers can model for children, families, and the larger community how to be lifelong learners when they share their thinking about an issue or topic, their questions, their decision-making processes, and even their mistakes. Additional similarities are outlined in "Some Similarities in Guiding Children and Guiding Adults" on the next page.

Some Similarities in Guiding Children and Guiding Adults

	Guiding Children	Guiding Adults
Relationships	Develops individual relationships with each child	Develops individual relationships with each staff member
Skills	Celebrates current skills	Recognizes and builds on current skills
Expectations	Conveys simple, age-appropriate expectations	Provides job descriptions and clear expectations
Emotions	Validates children's emotions and helps them to express their emotions appropriately	Listens to staff members' feelings and encourages a solution-oriented attitude
Conflict	Helps children learn to resolve conflict	Guides staff members to resolve conflict on their own and helps when necessary
Behavior	Redirects children to appropriate behavior	Coaches staff members to meet job expectations
Self-Sufficiency	Gives children opportunities to learn self-help skills	Delegates to help staff members become more self-sufficient

From *Being a Supervisor: Winning Ways for Early Childhood Professionals*, by Gigi Schweikert. Copyright © 2014. Reprinted with permission of Redleaf Press, St. Paul, MN; www.redleafpress.org.

Give Yourself the Permission to Lead

Many program directors never intended to be in the role. Quite a few are classroom teachers who became very knowledgeable about the program and advanced over time to lead it. Some directors are placed in the position at the request of their program boards; others are asked to step in during transitional periods or emergency circumstances. In cases like these, directors often find it hard to lead a group of individuals who have been their peers. As a classroom teacher, you are trained to be warm and nurturing at all times, and you work hard to build the trust and respect of children and families. But while directors should likewise be approachable and supportive, they also need to be authoritative, confident decision makers—whether it makes everyone happy or not.

Building partnerships with staff and exercising facilitative leadership are important, but to fulfill all of your different responsibilities, you must give yourself the permission to lead and act with authority in your role. Though pointed out earlier in this chapter, it bears repeating: being an effective director requires striking the right balance between good management and good leadership. Neither directors nor teachers want authority to be the only aspect of their work relationships. Most people want—and greatly benefit from—boss–employee interactions that are grounded in human connection and motivation, and research shows that when employees have a more personal relationship with their boss, it improves their level of engagement in their work (Anitha 2014; Artz 2013).

> **Directly from a Director**
>
> I never thought I would be a director. I always loved kids and my job as a classroom teacher, and I wasn't looking for something else. But when an opportunity presented itself, I thought, "I can do that job." I took the leap and never looked back. While some days the challenges are more difficult than I bargained for, overall I have found the rewards of supporting teachers and creating a center-based system, organization, and community that goes beyond one classroom deeply satisfying . . . and certainly never boring!

You can build your effectiveness as a leader by following these three essentials (Hill & Lineback 2011):

> ⟩ **Manage yourself.** Formal authority alone does not motivate or influence people. Instead, model the kind of behavior you expect from your staff. Be a leader they trust and want to emulate. For example, when listening to a teacher express a concern, model active listening and acknowledge his concern. Invite his thoughts on solutions and contribute thoughtful responses.

> **Manage your network.** Familiarize yourself with the roles, needs, and expectations of your staff, the program's board members, the families you serve, and the community. For example, be sure to make time to understand the role of each of the program's constituents and to meet with them as often as necessary to maintain a collaborative relationship.

> **Manage your team.** Think about the individual performance of teachers and staff who report to you and how you can inspire and empower them to be their best by supporting and fostering their goals and professional development. Promoting a high-performing "we" will lead to an effective, high-quality program. (Chapter 7 discusses this in more detail.) For example, engage teachers by offering a goal sheet at the beginning of each year on which they list things they want to accomplish in the classroom and as part of their professional growth. Check in at least once during the school year to see how things are going, and ask what resources you could provide that would help them accomplish their aims. At the end of the year, discuss what went well and what could be improved.

Directly from a Director

My problem is that I want my staff to like me. I have never been good at being a "boss." That's why during staff meetings, I use the state licensing regulations and NAEYC guidelines to justify my decisions. I tell my staff, "This is best practice. This is what we need to achieve." I want to get better at being a strong leader without falling back on a larger organization for support.

As you build a solid foundation in these areas, your confidence in your ability to make intentional decisions and to lead with purpose will grow.

Recognize What You Really Have Control Over

It is easy to become overwhelmed by the sheer number of responsibilities and problems you face on a daily basis. Each person who comes to you with a concern can often make it seem that *her* dilemma is the most pressing issue for you to address and resolve. Some problems are clear cut and relatively straightforward, while others are more complex. So, what should the director do to effectively prioritize and respond to issues? Start by considering these two points:

> **Clarify your role.** Ask what the person (or situation) needs or wants from you: A quick yes or no answer? A specific resource? Advice on what to do next? Simply a good listener?

> **Clarify your limitations.** What can you do to help resolve the problem? What can't you do? What do you have control over? What is out of your hands?

Knowing your role and your limitations can help you prioritize and focus your time and energy where it will be most effective. The following vignette illustrates how being mindful of these two points helps the director determine if and how she should act:

Zoya, a kindergarten teacher, walks into Melissa's office before the children arrive, shuts the door behind her, and begins to cry. Melissa is alarmed, wondering if there is a concern with a child or if Zoya is having an issue with a colleague. Her immediate priority is to find out the problem and to help Zoya regain her composure. If the issue is complex, it might require further conversations with Zoya, but for now, Melissa must try to help her return to the classroom to begin her responsibilities for the day.

She expresses concern and asks what is happening. Zoya confides that her home life has been very stressful lately; she and her husband have been fighting about finances.

"I'm so sorry to hear that," says Melissa, offering Zoya a tissue. "How can I help you?"

Zoya asks about her salary and if there is the possibility of a raise. Melissa knows that she does not have the authority to decide this, and she replies that she will reach out to the board for more information about the budget allocation plans for teacher salaries in the coming year. She also offers to meet with Zoya after school later in the week so they can take the time to discuss her concerns in more detail. With a plan in place and after talking a bit more with Melissa, Zoya calms down and returns to her classroom to get ready for the day.

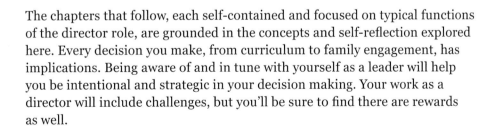

The chapters that follow, each self-contained and focused on typical functions of the director role, are grounded in the concepts and self-reflection explored here. Every decision you make, from curriculum to family engagement, has implications. Being aware of and in tune with yourself as a leader will help you be intentional and strategic in your decision making. Your work as a director will include challenges, but you'll be sure to find there are rewards as well.

Big-Picture Takeaways

> Directors are both managers and leaders. They must tend to managerial functions while bringing these functions into focus with the program's shared vision, mission, and goal.

> Leading adults is grounded in many of the same techniques used in working with children.

> Directors develop collaborative partnerships with staff and families so there is a shared, collective voice in planning, decision making, and implementation.

> Don't be afraid of being an authoritative figure. Effective leading means being a confident decision maker

> Every decision you make as a program leader needs to be intentional. Lead with vision and purpose.

Go Deeper

The Director's Toolbox (series), by P.J. Bloom (New Horizons, 2007–2016)

Five Elements of Collective Leadership for Early Childhood Professionals, by C. O'Neill and M. Brinkerhoff (Redleaf Press; NAEYC, 2017)

What You Need to Lead an Early Childhood Program: Emotional Intelligence in Practice, by H.E. Bruno (NAEYC, 2012)

Chapter Two

Program Context and Culture

In diversity there is beauty and there is strength. We all should know that diversity makes for a rich tapestry, and we must understand that all the threads of the tapestry are equal in value no matter their color.

—**Maya Angelou**, *Rainbow in the Cloud: The Wisdom and Spirit of Maya Angelou*

An early childhood program is a complex system of people, relationships, resources, barriers, possibilities, and dynamics. To be the most effective and responsive director you can be, you must develop an understanding of your program—what it is today, how it got that way, the individuals who have helped shape it, and its nuances, strengths, and areas of weakness. This understanding will enable you to foster the changes you think are needed. Because every program is different, there are no quick answers or simple solutions for instituting improvements. As a strategic director, you need to make decisions about where to put your energy, what is going to be the most effective route to your goals and objectives, and the speed at which to proceed.

Reading and Understanding the Context of Your Program

The metaphor of "reading" a program, adapted from Paulo Freire (1985), stands for the process of gathering and analyzing information about the program that will inform the changes you want to foster and help you map out a route to get there. You can discover much of this information by observing and assessing the program on a periodic or ongoing basis, but focused conversations with staff, families, board members, community members, and colleagues outside your program can also provide valuable insights. Involving others in this process gives you a variety of perspectives and can also help you nurture working relationships that are built on mutual trust and respect.

Consider the program from a historical perspective as well. In what areas has the program previously been successful? What has not been successful? Speaking with families, staff, and others who have been with the program for some time can provide you with helpful—and ideally, actionable—insights.

As Freire explains, "People must find themselves in the emerging leaders, and the latter must find themselves in the people" (1970, 163). That is to say, a leader cannot assume that she is the sole holder of information. When you talk with people about the program, keep in mind that you may not know as much as they do, and strive to have open dialogues in which you are willing to listen to other perspectives you may not have considered. When you invite families, staff, and others in the wider community to share their knowledge with you, your leadership role can begin to feel inclusive rather than overwhelming or isolating. Some steps you can take to read and understand your program are discussed over the next few pages.

Gather Information

The first step is to gather some preliminary impressions of your program by examining the following:

> **History.** Has the program been part of the fabric of the community for generations, or is it newly developed? Is it privately owned, corporate, or nonprofit? Is it large or small? Does it operate half days or full days?

> **Program culture.** What shared values and beliefs characterize the program? How have these changed over time? What traditions and practices make it unique?

> **Philosophy.** Does the program have a particular educational approach or philosophy (e.g., Reggio Emilia, Montessori, outdoor education, language immersion)? How has this changed over time?

> **Demographics.** Who are the children and families? What are their cultures and backgrounds? What is the gender, socioeconomic, and age makeup of the children? Are children with disabilities included? Who are the teachers? What level of training do they hold? How many years have they been in the classroom?

> **Stakeholders.** Who are the program's stakeholders? What are their roles? How have previous directors interacted and collaborated with them? What expectations do they have for the program and for the director?

> **Resources.** What particular resources does the program have at its disposal (e.g., university or community partnerships, grants, teachers or families with specialized expertise)? How are these resources used? What untapped resources might exist?

Analyze the Information

Once you feel you have gathered a substantial amount of information about your program, tease out what the data suggest. It may help to start by identifying the following:

> **Strengths and needs.** What are the program's strongest attributes (e.g., high family engagement, teachers who go above and beyond expectations)? What aspects require attention and improvement (e.g., children with physical disabilities cannot easily navigate the building, enrollment has been declining over the past several years)? Which of these needs is most urgent to address?

> **Allies.** Look for administrators, teachers, families, community members, and friends who support the program, its philosophical approach, and its curriculum goals. Who are your current and potential allies? What kind of support, connections, or opportunities can your allies offer (e.g., volunteer time, fundraising event venue, donated supplies, exposure to a new audience, discounted advertising space)?

> **Gatekeepers.** Gatekeepers are people or groups who oversee a program's operation by virtue of their institutional position or role (Derman-Sparks, LeeKeenan, & Nimmo 2015). Who are the gatekeepers in your program (e.g., sponsoring organization, regulators)? What are they invested in? What initiatives have they supported or opposed in the past? How can you maintain open channels of communication with them?

> **Opportunities.** Being responsive to situations as they arise and seeking the opportunities in each has the potential to fuel your program's mission and goals. For example, if licensing or accreditation is up for renewal, it may be a good time to move forward with pending revisions to your family handbook or family intake forms. Or, if several new hires express confusion about the program's child assessment and portfolio system, that might be the impetus to involve staff in reviewing and simplifying a cumbersome process.

> **Obstacles.** A variety of factors can slow, complicate, or stall your plans for program improvement. Some obstacles can be anticipated, while others cannot. Keep an open mind, use creative problem solving, and be flexible with your goals and plans to help reduce—or even eliminate—a number of obstacles that might at first seem insurmountable. For example, as part of your program's emphasis on improving family engagement, you want to provide food and child care services for families so they can attend family–teacher conferences and meetings. However, there aren't funds for this in the budget. How might you reframe this obstacle as an opportunity? Perhaps a local supermarket or restaurant would be willing to donate food for meetings. Maybe students at your local community college could provide child care as part of their fieldwork. Consider helping families organize and take turns watching each other's children at the center during conferences.

Set Program Goals and Develop an Action Plan

Based on the information you have gathered and analyzed, identify some short- and long-term goals. To help you stay on track, limit yourself to three long-term goals at a time. Outline specific steps for each of these goals. Make the short-term goals realistic, aligning them with concrete objectives. Especially for long-term goals, it is helpful to develop a timeline and commit to checking on the progress. "Itty Bitty Academy's Playground Improvement Plan" on the next page illustrates a sample timeline a director might create for plotting out a long-term goal with action steps.

Itty Bitty Academy's
Playground Improvement Plan

Problem
The program's outdoor crawl tunnel is getting old and worn, and it will need to be replaced within the next year or two. This will be a significant expense.

Goal
To secure board approval and obtain the funds to replace the crawl tunnel by the end of next spring

Timeline for Action Steps

June	Review current regulations regarding outdoor play spaces and equipment. Research estimates for replacing the crawl tunnel.
July	Notify the staff and administration of your interest in replacing the crawl tunnel. Share what you've learned so far, and ask for input on options they would like considered (e.g., purchasing another crawl tunnel, purchasing a different piece of play equipment or materials the children can manipulate and construct with, hiring a construction team to build a new piece of equipment).
August	Assess how much is currently in the budget for this improvement, and generate a list of fundraising ideas to cover remaining expenses.
September	Announce to the school community the program's interest in removing the old crawl tunnel from the playground and replacing it with new play equipment. Collect ideas and feedback from children, families, staff, and the community. Organize a volunteer group of families and community members to explore additional fundraising ideas.
October	Research playground vendors and get quotes for the cost of a new piece of play equipment.
November	Based on constituent feedback, determine what equipment will replace the crawl tunnel and confirm the funding needed.
December–February	Oversee aggressive fundraising to meet the fiscal goal for the equipment.
March	Hire an installation or construction team.
April	Restrict children's access to the playground during the installation (or construction) of the new play equipment.
May	Hold a playground reopening celebration for the children, families, staff, board members, and everyone involved in the improvement project, including funders and construction workers.

Creating and Cultivating the Culture of Your Program

A program's culture is characterized by a number of things, including its mission, shared values and beliefs, expectations, goals, and the way it is organized. The culture of a program can be created by top-down (director-driven) or bottom-up (constituent-driven) approaches, or a combination of the two. Directors influence and shape the culture of early childhood education programs in many ways, and it is the director's responsibility to communicate the culture of the program in a cohesive way that everyone can agree on. A program's culture should be dynamic and responsive to changing needs, but there are some qualities that are intrinsically tied to a healthy, positive culture based on openness, trust, and respect.

Strong Relationships

As director, it is essential that you nurture relationships with families, children, and teachers. Positive relationships do not just happen; they must be built over time through interactions that are authentic, reciprocal, and mutually respectful. Make time for your entire school community—the more intentional, consistent, and organized this time is, the easier it will be to make it a regular part of your schedule and something others can depend on.

The director is often the person to whom families turn when concerns, questions, or challenges arise with their children in the classroom. For such interactions to be successful, it helps immensely to have already created a positive relationship with a family. When connecting with families, small gestures can go a long way toward building trust and mutual understanding. Families need to see you as a critical and visual part of the school community. Here are a few simple suggestions:

> Be present at the school entrance every day at arrival and departure times to greet families.

> Keep your office door open as much as possible. This signals to families that they are welcome to stop by anytime, not just when there is a problem. For more formal meetings, provide a consistent schedule of times when families are welcome to meet with you.

> Coordinate creative events that bring the program community together in a personal way.

> Offer special director talks monthly to your program community to discuss current topics of interest in early childhood. If possible, provide refreshments for families at these events.

While teachers handle the bulk of the daily classroom-based interactions with children, children need to see *you* in their classrooms frequently to feel connected to you. Make an effort to spend time working and playing with the children.

> Keep a consistent weekly schedule of when you will visit classrooms to interact with the children. Work with the teachers to find times that fit with their routines.

> Be a visiting reader or join a class for lunch or snack time.

> Organize a special activity during an important school celebration so children can interact with you directly.

> Join a field trip.

Your relationship with each staff member affects the way the school community works and how other relationships are approached. Below are just a few ideas for conveying acceptance and respect and for building trust with teachers:

> Make yourself accessible to staff, just as you do to families. This goes a long way toward demonstrating that you care about staff members' needs, interests, and input.

> Create staff meeting rituals that encourage sharing and camaraderie; for example, when a new teacher joins the program, arrange some getting-to-know-you icebreakers everyone can participate in (e.g., sharing where your name comes from, your favorite children's book growing up and why).

> Coordinate the occasional staff potluck breakfast or dinner.

> Organize an annual staff-only retreat.

> Dedicate a comfortable space in the building where staff can meet, prepare materials, and talk without disruption.

> Celebrate staff birthdays.

> Validate and reward staff with small notes or tokens of appreciation in their mailboxes. Find out how each staff member prefers to be recognized or shown appreciation.

> Provide a suggestion box with paper and pens in a prominent place. Compile a list of the suggestions you receive each week and respond briefly to them at a staff meeting. You don't need to implement every suggestion, but show that you are open to and value input and new ideas.

Meaningful and Effective Communication

Communication is a key component of social and educational experiences. For communication to be both meaningful and effective, interactions among all individuals who have a stake in the program must be clear, timely, and reciprocal. The director is the hub of this communication network. You must develop and implement communication strategies that are "frequent, personal, and consistent" (Powell 1998, 65). However, avoid overloading staff with so many communications that they find it difficult to know which are really important (Bloom, Hentschel, & Bella 2016). Consider what staff need to know from you and the most effective method of communicating that information. During a staff meeting? In a weekly memo? In more intimate discussions with each teaching team?

Chapters 7 and 8 discuss a few communication strategies to use with staff and families, respectively, in more detail. When you model respectful and supportive communication skills, teachers and families are likely to follow suit. The most effective staffs communicate and operate as a professional team so that they can offer the best care and education to children.

A Welcoming Environment

The environment of a program is an important part of the culture, and it's made up of many layers. Physical spaces—classrooms, hallways, offices, outdoor spaces, and common areas—should be comfortable for the people who spend time there. Make sure there is child-size furniture in all areas where children are and adult-size seating and work space for staff and families. The physical environment should also be intentionally designed to reflect the diversity of the community your program serves. Incorporate materials like photographs, books, art, and music that portray a variety of cultures, languages, abilities, family structures, geographical regions, and religions. Every child and family should feel like they belong. When children or family members see themselves reflected in the environment and the curriculum, they feel safe, valued, and welcome.

Culture Versus Climate

Culture and climate may seem like the same thing, but while these two concepts share some characteristics, they are critically different. *Culture* reflects the expectations of a program, made visible in the way things are done—the practices that arise out of the program's beliefs, values, norms, and relationships. For example, a program might value two-way feedback between the director and staff members and build in several formal and informal ways of providing this feedback.

In contrast, *climate* is often described as the "feel" of the program—its atmosphere. Some programs radiate positive energy and have a welcoming feeling, even to first-time visitors. In other programs, the climate may be more businesslike—more corporate or even competitive. Climate reflects the collective attitude of staff toward the program's beliefs, values, and norms.

Bloom (2016) outlines 10 dimensions that make up organizational climate, including these:

> **Supervisor support** refers to the clear expectations, encouragement, feedback, and other resources you provide staff members so they can be effective. For example, when you listen carefully to a teacher's concerns and respond to them in a timely manner, she is likely to feel validated and positive about her working environment.

> **Goal consensus** is the extent to which staff agree on the philosophy and goals of the program. For example, at the beginning of the program year, you might provide opportunities for staff to review the program's mission statement and educational objectives together and conduct an honest dialogue about them. Returning teachers might offer examples of what the program philosophy looks like in practice and discuss their views on collective goal progress. New staff members can contribute their ideas and also ask questions for clarification. This process provides transparency, greater understanding, and consensus about the program's direction.

> **Innovativeness** refers to openness to change, willingness to adapt and try new things, and ability to engage in creative problem solving. The adage "Change is inevitable, but growth is optional" comes to mind. You can foster a spirit of innovation and creativity by encouraging staff to try something new in the classroom or brainstorm ways to learn about and tap into families' skills and talents. Encourage openness to change by helping staff see change as an opportunity to try something new. For example, if new fire safety regulations limit the number of paper wall displays allowed in the classroom, encourage teachers to problem solve new ways to display children's work— maybe they'll decide to put together digital classroom portfolios, use clips to hang artwork from wire strung across the room, or display the work in shadow boxes and acrylic frames.

It is often easier to change a program's climate than it is to change its culture. However, if the organizational climate is adjusted slowly over time, culture can change too.

It is also important to consider the emotional tone and atmosphere of your program's environment. Beyond making the physical environment welcoming for all families, how does the staff act toward them? Does a family whose child frequently exhibits challenging behavior nevertheless feel the staff's acceptance of the child and their interest in her unique personality? How do staff members treat each other? Think about what you already do that fosters a positive atmosphere and how you might improve this aspect of your program.

Risk Taking, Reflection, and Growth

As mentioned in Chapter 1, effective directors are facilitative leaders who partner with teachers to improve program processes and policies. Part of building these partnerships means establishing a culture where you and your staff members feel comfortable trying new ideas, taking carefully considered risks, and using mistakes to learn, reflect, and grow. One way to start a conversation with teachers about taking new risks is to set aside time to discuss aspects of their jobs that are challenging for them. For example, is there a child who always seems to push their emotional buttons? Do they struggle to develop vigorous but safe physical activities for children to engage in indoors?

A Word About Anti-Bias Education

We live in an increasingly diverse and global world. NAEYC clearly states that "early childhood programs are responsible for creating a welcoming environment that respects diversity, supports children's ties to their families and community, and promotes both second language acquisition and preservation of children's home languages and cultural identities" (2009, 1). In addition to embracing cultural and linguistic diversity, we emphasize that programs expand this position to more broadly encompass all kinds of differences, such as family structure, sexual orientation, ability, class, socioeconomic status, gender, race, and religion.

Anti-bias education is an approach that provides practical guidance for educators on confronting and eliminating barriers of prejudice, misinformation, and bias (Derman-Sparks, LeeKeenan, & Nimmo 2015). A program grounded in anti-bias education puts diversity and equity goals at the center of all aspects of its organization and daily life, from setting up the center and classroom environment to developing curriculum to interacting with children and families. This philosophy is not just about adding new materials to an existing learning environment; it involves systemic changes in a program's mission, policies, procedures, and professional development to ensure equity and opportunity and to make sure everyone's voice is heard. It provides a framework to value and create a community that supports and seeks to include all dimensions of human difference.

For a more comprehensive overview on implementing anti-bias education in your program, check out *Leading Anti-Bias Early Childhood Programs: A Guide for Change* (Derman-Sparks, LeeKeenan, & Nimmo 2015).

Directors need to create safe spaces to have these conversations. Just as teachers do for children in the classroom, directors can set some ground rules to create a safe space for open discussion and collaboration with staff. Here are some examples of helpful ground rules:

> Engage in active listening.

> Don't make assumptions.

> Be honest.

> Speak from your own experience.

> Be respectful.

> Value all questions.

Revisit these ground rules throughout the year to revise and add to them as needed (Derman-Sparks, LeeKeenan, & Nimmo 2015).

Teachers might come to you interested—yet anxious—to step out of their comfort zone by setting up a makerspace in their classroom, using puppets to introduce sensitive topics that are affecting the children, changing the schedule to consistently include small group activities so they can focus more on individual children, inviting a family member they've had limited interactions with to come to read a book to the children, or even teaching creative movement for the first time. In these situations, do you encourage them to think through their idea and then try it? Be aware of the effect your words, tone, body language, and enthusiasm (or lack of) can have on your staff's desire to stretch themselves and the children.

By encouraging teachers to reflect on their practice—including what they feel they do well, what they might do differently, and why they think a particular change would benefit the children—you will help them feel more empowered to take these risks. You can also model risk taking by sharing some of the challenges and questions you have faced as director and how you used them as learning opportunities for professional and personal growth. This kind of openness allows the teachers to feel that it's okay to make mistakes and that they can learn from them.

The following vignette illustrates a director taking a risk and sharing it with her staff.

> Martin Luther King, Jr., Day is approaching, and Donna, the director of a learning center for children birth to age 5, really wants to recognize the important contributions of Martin Luther King, Jr. She feels strongly that young children understand the concepts of justice and fairness. However, as a White woman, she isn't sure it would be appropriate for her to take the lead in a discussion about civil rights, especially in a predominantly Black school community.

Donna decides to first reach out to a few Black teachers at the center as well as some families in the school and colleagues in her network to hear their thoughts on the best way for her to approach her predominately White staff about discussing civil rights with preschool children. The staff members and colleagues she reaches out to give her encouraging and constructive feedback, even offering to share some of the activities they do with the children with the rest of her staff.

During the next staff meeting, Donna notes that Martin Luther King, Jr., Day is coming up and that it offers an important opportunity to talk about justice and fairness with the children. She shares some of the ideas her colleagues had suggested and then invites the teachers to share curriculum activities they are aware of or have previously done on the topic. Donna encourages all the teachers to develop activities that explore justice and fairness.

Most of the teachers plan activities that help children think about making things fairer for everyone in their class or at home. At the next staff meeting, Donna encourages the teachers to continue pursuing the topic as the children show interest and ask questions. Afterward, many teachers and families approach Donna to say how happy they are that the school is showing its support for justice and fairness. Donna decides to look for additional ways to explore justice and fairness throughout the year.

Program context and culture may seem like abstract concepts, but they reflect the real, everyday factors that give your setting its unique appeal and make it a place everyone can feel a part of. As a program leader, your job is to work with staff and other stakeholders to set goals for the program and invite them to join you in making those goals a reality. This requires some risk taking, which is always part of the teaching and learning process. What risks do *you* need to take to spark excellence in your program?

Big-Picture Takeaways

> Learn about the context and history of your program, and the people associated with it, to understand how your program became what it is today and gain insight into how you can support its continuing development.

> Listen to your constituencies to better understand the program's strengths and needs and identify strategic short- and long-term goals.

> Build an inclusive culture for your center by facilitating strong relationships, communicating effectively, and providing a welcoming environment. Encourage risk taking, reflection, and growth as a part of the learning process for staff.

Go Deeper

"Disrupting Inequity" (*Educational Leadership* issue, Vol. 74, No. 3, November 2016)

Doing the Right Thing for Children: Eight Qualities of Leadership, by M. Sykes (Redleaf Press, 2014)

Leading Anti-Bias Early Childhood Programs: A Guide for Change, by L. Derman-Sparks, D. LeeKeenan, and J. Nimmo (Teachers College Press; NAEYC, 2015)

Chapter Three

Achieving and Maintaining Program Quality

Directors of early childhood programs can take steps to prevent problems from exploding into . . . disasters. The more preventive measures they take, the more confident and effective they become as leaders.

—Holly Elissa Bruno, *What You Need to Lead an Early Childhood Program: Emotional Intelligence in Practice*

Directly from a Director

Our vision is to create sustainable change in our center—not pie-in-the-sky change but change that will outlast any one individual.
This happens through building relationships with everyone— teachers, children, families, and beyond.

One of your most important responsibilities as a director is to ensure the quality of your program. *Quality* is defined in many ways using various criteria, including regulations and standards established at the local, state, and national levels. Understanding and meeting these regulations and standards is essential to ensuring and maintaining a high-quality early childhood program. Clear, well-developed program policies and procedures act as preventive measures and also provide guidance in times of crisis. This chapter will explore the director's role in managing program quality through the establishment and maintenance of policies and procedures, licensing, and accreditation. While time consuming, these processes are a valuable way to improve your program no matter where your starting point may be.

Developing Policies and Procedures

Written policies and procedures provide a framework of guidelines and expectations that clearly explain your program's services and regulations. They ensure that everyone in the program has a common set of rules that they are committed to following. While policies and procedures are often informed by the requirements of your licensing and quality assurance or accreditation agency, we'll begin by focusing on some fundamental topics that all early childhood program policies and procedures should address for staff and families.

Vision and Mission Statements

Every early childhood program should have both a vision statement and a mission statement. A program's vision statement encapsulates what the program wants to be and hopes to accomplish; it is the big-picture view of what you believe about your program and what you want to achieve. Use it to guide all actions you and the staff and other stakeholders take. If an action is not moving you toward your vision, you might do well to question why you are doing it.

The mission statement is tied to the vision statement and provides an operational scaffold for its work—a way to achieve the vision. As Derman-Sparks, LeeKeenan, and Nimmo explain, "While a vision statement expresses what you hope to accomplish, a mission statement describes the program's particular purpose and provides a framework for working toward the vision. [Together, these statements] act as inspiration and guide for a program's work,

laying the foundation for developing annual goals and educational objectives"
(2015, 25). As you draft a mission statement, continually refer back to the
vision statement to keep focused on where the program is headed.

It can take time, even years, to create vision and mission statements that feel
just right for your program. So where do you start? You might be the director
of a program that already has vision and mission statements in place, but
they feel outdated or don't reflect current understanding of best practices in
child development and learning. Or perhaps your program operates under a
sponsoring organization that has its own vision and mission statements. You
might start with those statements and refine them to more closely reflect your
program and how it fits into the sponsoring organization. Maybe your program
has a particular philosophy (e.g., Montessori method, Reggio Emilia approach)
but no vision or mission statement. In this case, you might use the program's
philosophy as a framework to develop them. In other cases, you may join a
program and find there are no statements or specific curriculum approach. For
any of these situations, here are some steps to guide you through the process of
developing or fine-tuning vision and mission statements. Because your mission
statement outlines how you will achieve your vision, begin with drafting the
vision statement.

1. **Establish what you want the program to achieve and how you will get there.** Spend some time thinking about what qualities you feel make a program successful and envisioning what you want to see in program. What would your ideal program look like? What will it take to get there? Carter and Curtis (2010) emphasize that an organization's vision cannot come from one person; rather, its development is a collaborative effort. This process should include discussion and input from staff, board members, the families you serve, and any sponsoring organization. In discussions about your mission statement, consider ways to know how you are achieving it. What will success look like?

2. **Do some research.** Review the vision and mission statements of other programs or organizations you value and admire. You might have access to other programs' handbooks or brochures, but you can typically find such statements on their websites too. Reach out to other directors you know to ask them about their programs' statements and how they were created. As part of this step, take notes on what you like and don't like about each statement you review. Are the values, goals, and philosophy clear? Is the statement easy to read and understand, free of educational jargon? Finally, review the *Code of Ethical Conduct and Statement of*

Example of a Program's Vision, Mission, and Goal

Learning Rainbow Early Childhood Education Center

Our Vision Statement

Learning Rainbow believes diversity is integral to the learning and development of all young children. All children and families deserve access to high-quality education and care in an inclusive, safe, and stimulating community.

Our Mission Statement

Learning Rainbow incorporates an anti-bias education stance in all aspects of our organization. We focus on providing learning opportunities that build on children's unique strengths and on developing strong relationships with children, families, and colleagues built on mutual respect and appreciation for different cultures, languages, values, and family structures.

Our Goal

Our goal is to create an environment and a robust curriculum that celebrate diversity; promote awareness and acceptance of both similarities and differences

Commitment (NAEYC 2016) to refamiliarize yourself with the values and principles of a morally responsible early childhood program. Keep in mind that both your vision and mission statements must be tailored to your own program. You may get inspiration from reading other programs' statements, but what does *your* program stand for? What does it value?

3. **Draft the vision or mission statement.** Based on the input and information you have gathered and the thoughtful consideration of what you and your stakeholders want your program to be, draft the vision or mission statement. Keep it clear and concise, always keeping in mind whether it articulates what you really believe (the vision statement) and helps you work toward your vision (the mission statement). Remember, a good vision or mission statement will be understood by the general public, not just educators. Most important, both should inform the way the center operates on a daily basis.

4. **Hold focus groups.** Share the drafted vision and mission statements with your stakeholders—staff, families, board members, alumni, other valued colleagues, and the community. As part of this vetting process, note both positive and critical feedback. Everyone must be fully invested in the same goals so that the statements are more than just lofty-sounding words.

Once you have vision and mission statements that feel true to your program, revisit them periodically with staff and families. Remember, the statements are living documents. You must *use* them as a framework and guide for decision making to determine if they work for your program. And, use the statements to inform the goals your program sets out to accomplish each year. (See "Example of a Program's Vision, Mission, and Goal" on the previous page.)

Organizational Chart

An organizational chart clearly delineates staff roles and responsibilities by illustrating whom each person reports to and can turn to with problems or concerns. Such charts are particularly important for large-scale programs or those with a complex structure.

To design an organizational chart, start by listing all the people in your program and their roles, such as the director, assistant director, administrative assistants, teachers, assistant teachers, parent coordinators, and any other full- and part-time staff. Then arrange the names of the roles in a vertical or horizontal flow chart that connects each to (1) the person they report to directly and (2) anyone who reports to them. Depending on the complexity of your program, it might be easiest to start from the top and work down, or vice versa. Two examples of organization charts, one for a program with a larger, more complex structure and one that is relatively small, can be seen on pages 32 and 33, respectively. There are also software programs, ranging in cost and ease of use, that can help you with this process. Make this chart easily visible and accessible to all staff by including it in the staff handbook and/or posting a copy on the staff bulletin board.

Sunnyside Early Education and Care Center at St. Hedwig's University Hospital (Large Program Organizational Chart)

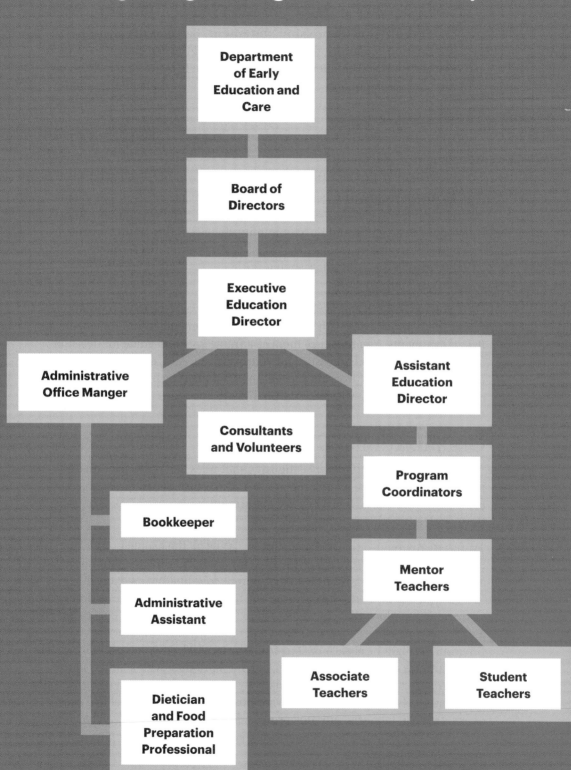

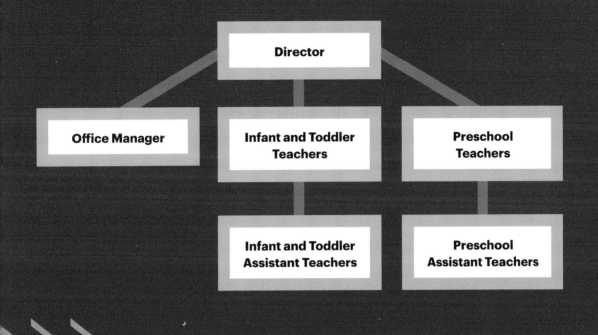

Starling Early Learning
(Small Program Organizational Chart)

Director

Office Manager

Infant and Toddler Teachers

Preschool Teachers

Infant and Toddler Assistant Teachers

Preschool Assistant Teachers

Safety Procedures

It's snack time in Alonso's classroom of 3- and 4-year-olds. He and his teacher assistant, Michaela, are sitting with the children at small tables, making conversation and keeping an eye out in case anyone needs help as they serve themselves fresh, cut-up fruit from the platters.

Suddenly Alonso hears one of the children begin to cough. He quickly crouches beside Velma as her coughing turns to strangled sounds and her face slowly turns red. Alonso is CPR/AED/Heimlich certified, as all teachers in the program are required to be, but he has never actually performed the Heimlich maneuver on someone who was choking.

While Michaela occupies the other children, Alonso quickly glances at the Heimlich maneuver diagram poster that is displayed prominently in the snack area, assuring himself of how to position the child's body and his own arms. He performs each step of the maneuver on Velma, and by the second abdominal thrust, Velma spits up the cube of cantaloupe that had been lodged in her throat.

Once Alonso comforts Velma and is sure she is breathing without difficulty and no longer in danger of choking, he calls the director on the internal phone system to inform her of the incident and to ask her to have the program nurse, who is in the building that day, come to the room. Then he calls Velma's mother to let her know what has happened.

National, state, and local regulations provide criteria to ensure that early care and education centers are safe places for children and staff. Without first aid training, Alonso would not have known what to do in a choking emergency. In addition, staff are required to have a criminal background check before they can be employed as a caregiver or educator of children. Other safety guidelines and particulars are up to the director to develop and update, such as requiring first aid kits to be available in all classrooms and posting emergency numbers and instructions on all classroom bulletin boards. Protocols for ongoing safety drills may be developed in conjunction with the local fire and police departments. Once comprehensive emergency management plans for natural disasters or other emergency situations requiring evacuation of building are established, the evacuation process must be practiced periodically. Some, like fire drills, must be practiced on a more regular basis with monitoring by the fire marshals; others, like sheltering in place, are done less frequently without supervision from external safety enforcing authorities.

Identifying and Reporting Suspected Child Neglect and Abuse

Francesca approaches her program director, Zachary, after school one day to discuss a concern she has about one of the children in her class. Over the last several days, 5-year-old Stevie, a normally lively child, has been withdrawn and only interested in drawing explicit images about her body that seem to depict people touching her inappropriately. As recommended by the program's policies, Francesca has carefully documented these behaviors and finds them unusual enough to feel she has reasonable cause to suspect sexual abuse. Zachary agrees with her assessment, and they contact the local child protective services agency to file a report.

As professionals who work with young children, early childhood educators are *mandated reporters*—that is, they are required by law to report any suspicions of physical or sexual child abuse or neglect (Child Welfare Information Gateway 2016). It is crucial to educate staff about your state's regulations on child abuse and neglect, including

> Identifying signs of abuse

> Documenting observations and concerns

> Submitting a report to the appropriate authorities

Teachers are empowered by law to make a report on their own; they may consult with their director first but are not required to do so. Your staff should understand that if one of them reports suspected abuse in the program, he is immune from discharge or retaliation unless it turns out the report was malicious. Staff must be assured that they can report a situation that could potentially pose difficulties for the program. The child's safety is of the utmost importance.

If you or another program constituent suspects a staff member of child abuse or neglect, child protective services and the appropriate licensing authorities must be notified immediately. Based on these authorities' regulations, your policies should also outline how the program will act if a staff member is suspected of child abuse while the investigation is being conducted (e.g., an enforced leave of absence, removed from contact with children and given other duties) and beyond (e.g., former duties reinstated if cleared of charges, terminated if found guilty).

Having these policies clearly defined in writing and sharing them with staff and families can help everyone better understand the program's obligations when it comes to safety and well-being of the children.

Guidance and Discipline

Clear, consistent, and developmentally appropriate approaches to foster children's social skills and emotional well-being should be outlined for staff. Consider children with a variety of needs, such as children with disabilities and those who need more movement and activity in their daily routine. Teachers need support and time to confer with you and colleagues about effective ways to build the skills children need to be emotionally healthy and develop positive relationships with other children and adults, such as self-regulation, working collaboratively with peers, and ignoring distractions and staying focused on a task. Stay up to date on research findings about brain development and the effects of stress, including adverse childhood experiences and toxic stress, on children's development and behavior. Engage teachers in discussions about these findings so they can better understand the types of guidance and support children need and why.

Effective guidance strategies help children develop the skills they need to be successful in school and in life. Emphasize to teachers that strategies should be used *not* to punish children but to help them understand their emotions, the effects of their actions on themselves and others, and ways they can begin to regulate their own behavior. In addition, encourage teachers to set up the classroom environment so that it helps children become more independent and successful. A clear, predictable routine is an important aspect of a supportive classroom environment. "Children thrive and learn best in settings where they feel connected and safe" (Howell & Reinhard 2015, 9).

As you develop or review your program's curriculum or approach, be sure that it includes a research-based social and emotional learning component that reflects your vision and mission and the needs of the children in your program.

The Collaborative for Academic, Social, and Emotional Learning (CASEL) offers information and suggestions for selecting effective social and emotional learning programs.

The past 10 years have seen high rates of expulsion and suspension in early childhood programs (HHS & ED 2016). This trend is troubling for a number of reasons. Expulsion and suspension are linked to a number of short- and long-term negative consequences for children, including an increased likelihood of dropping out of school, academic failure, and incarceration (HHS & ED 2016). Furthermore, there are racial- and gender-based disparities evident in expulsion rates. Data suggest that biased perceptions and implementation of disciplinary policies and practices may be leading to specific groups of children, primarily young boys of color, being more likely to be expelled or suspended than their peers (HHS & ED 2016).

All stakeholders should know your program's guidelines on suspension and expulsion. In developing and implementing these guidelines, consider the 2016 joint policy statement by the US Departments of Health and Human Services (HHS) and of Education (ED) on suspension and expulsion. The policy states

> Early childhood programs are strongly encouraged to establish policies that eliminate or severely limit expulsion, suspension, or other exclusionary discipline; these exclusionary measures should be used only as a last resort in extraordinary circumstances where there is a determination of a serious safety threat that cannot otherwise be reduced or eliminated by the provision of reasonable modifications. (HHS & ED 2016, 2)

We urge using the following recommendations from HHS and ED (2016) as guidelines:

> Develop and clearly communicate preventive guidance and discipline practices to staff and families.

> Develop and clearly communicate expulsion and suspension policies.

> Provide resources to strengthen your staff's skills in supporting children's social and emotional health and addressing challenging behavior.

> Seek support from experts, such as mental health consultants and behavioral specialists.

> Promote health and wellness among your staff; teacher stress has been shown to predict suspensions and expulsions.

> Set goals, such as increasing staff access to specialists and decreasing suspensions and expulsions by a certain percentage over each of the next few years. Collect and analyze data to assess progress toward these goals.

> Make use of free resources to enhance staff training and strengthen partnerships with families.

Staff and Family Handbooks

While many of your policies will be visible in a number of places—accreditation portfolios, family bulletin boards, and classrooms, just to name a few—typically, the most comprehensive source will be your program's staff and family handbooks. The staff handbook contains all the policies and procedures required for staff. Examples are personnel policies about benefits and salary, policies and procedures about safety, teaching responsibilities, curriculum implementation, and child assessment procedures. The family handbook contains policies and procedures that families need to know to be members of the center's community, such as health regulations, food policies, attendance policies, and family participation guidelines. Many of the same policies are relevant for both staff and families and are included in both handbooks. A more comprehensive list of criteria for policies and procedures that are often covered in these handbooks as well as those typically required for licensing and accreditation can be found in the "Sample Criteria for Policies and Procedures, Licensing, and Accreditation" chart on pages 38–39. Keep in mind that these criteria vary widely across programs, states, and accrediting bodies, so the criteria pertinent to your own program may vary from what is displayed in the chart.

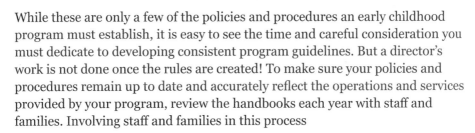

While these are only a few of the policies and procedures an early childhood program must establish, it is easy to see the time and careful consideration you must dedicate to developing consistent program guidelines. But a director's work is not done once the rules are created! To make sure your policies and procedures remain up to date and accurately reflect the operations and services provided by your program, review the handbooks each year with staff and families. Involving staff and families in this process

> Gives them the opportunity to suggest topics that might not be addressed or are addressed in ways that feel contradictory to the program's mission statement

> Helps you understand how staff and families interpret the information provided and whether clarification is needed

> Offers additional perspectives on whether the policies and procedures are as supportive and inclusive as possible

Keep in mind that while there are common elements across all early childhood program policies and procedures, these guidelines will also reflect the unique diversity stemming from each program's children, families, staff, and community.

Sample Criteria for Policies and Procedures, Licensing, and Accreditation

	Typically Required for Licensing and Accreditation	Typically Required for Staff Handbook	Typically Required for Family Handbook
General Information			
Mission statement	Yes	Yes	Yes
Organizational chart	Sometimes	Yes	Yes
Board roster	Yes	Yes	Yes
Audited financial statement	Yes	No	No
Enrollment and staff lists for each age group served (child–teacher ratios)	Yes	Yes	Yes
Curriculum			
Curriculum philosophy and learning goals	Yes	Yes	Yes
Daily lesson plans and developmental activity plans	Yes	Yes	Yes
Daily schedule	Yes	Yes	Yes
Accommodations and adaptations for children with disabilities	Yes	Yes	Yes
Child assessment plan progress reports and family–teacher conferences	Yes	Yes	Yes
Equipment and materials lists	Yes	Yes	Yes
Staff Information			
Qualifications			
Job descriptions	Yes	Yes	No
Resumes	Yes	Yes	No
Professional licenses	Yes	Yes	No
References and background checks	Yes	Yes	No
Personnel Policies			
Hiring process	Yes	Yes	No
Nondiscriminatory statement	Yes	Yes	No
Benefits	Yes	Yes	No
Personnel records	Yes	Yes	No
Attendance	Yes	Yes	No

	Typically Required for Licensing and Accreditation	Typically Required for Staff Handbook	Typically Required for Family Handbook

Staff Information (continued)

Personnel Policies (continued)

Grievance	Yes	Yes	No
Performance evaluation	Yes	Yes	No
Employee conduct and discipline policy	Yes	Yes	No
Termination	Yes	Yes	No

Professional Development

Orientation	Yes	Yes	No
Supervision plan	Yes	Yes	No
Trainings	Yes	Yes	No
Staff meeting schedule	Sometimes	Yes	No

Child and Family Information

Enrollment and withdrawal	Yes	Yes	Yes
Anti-bias/anti-discrimination stance	Yes	Yes	Yes
Child records	Sometimes	Yes	Yes
Attendance and absenteeism	Yes	Yes	Yes
Arrival and departure	Yes	Yes	Yes
Guidance, behavior management, and discipline	Yes	Yes	Yes
Identifying and reporting child abuse and neglect	Yes	Yes	Yes
Menus, food plans, and nutrition	Yes	Yes	Yes
Health policies	Yes	Yes	Yes
Comprehensive emergency management plans	Yes	Yes	Yes
Transportation	Yes	Yes	Yes
Field trip policies	Sometimes	Yes	Yes
Family engagement and participation	Sometimes	Yes	Yes
Family conduct	Yes	Yes	Yes

Directly from a Director

Sometimes it feels like children's opportunities for creative free play are being overregulated. However, on the other side, the regulations guide us, push us, and back us up.

Even after you have written, reviewed, and made public the policies and procedures that govern your program, there are no guarantees that the staff and families will follow them. Many directors do, however, require their staff and families to sign a statement acknowledging they have read and agree to follow the policies and procedures outlined in the handbook.

Orientation meetings for newly hired staff are great opportunities to discuss key and more complicated policies in detail, such as how to communicate policy issues or address conflicts with families. Similarly, when families enroll their children in the program, you might hold a family orientation meeting to share the program's policies. Allow time for families to bring up questions, comments, or concerns they may have. If there are certain policies that have recently changed, are frequently misunderstood, or will soon be of particular relevance, consider highlighting and explaining them in your program newsletter or another type of communication. You can never communicate and reiterate important information too many times or in too many different ways!

Licensing Basics

Every local and state government has licensing requirements for the operation of an early childhood education program to ensure that safe, healthy practices are followed. Licensure is necessary for the legal operation of a center and ensures only that minimum requirements have been met. Licensing rules and regulations are unique to each state, and they often change in response to current research, monetary considerations, and politics. Some licensing agencies have separate requirements for different types of settings (private, publicly funded, religiously sponsored, family child care programs), while others treat all programs in the same manner. Though requirements vary, there are some universal elements you can expect to be addressed.

Physical Space

Licensing criteria address indoor and outdoor facilities, design (including Americans with Disabilities Act [ADA] accessibility compliance), furniture, equipment, materials, and environmental health. For example, state regulations often define the square footage required for the number of children in a specific classroom, as well as specific measurements for furniture to ensure it is sized for children in the age ranges the program serves. State regulations also stipulate safety and supervision guidelines for things like installation of *fall zones*—the area surrounding gross motor play equipment where protective surfacing or fill materials (e.g., sand, recycled rubber mulch, pea gravel) is required to prevent children from being hurt if they fall.

Staff Education and Training Requirements

While state regulations vary on the minimum qualifications for early childhood teachers, most identify a specific number of hours required annually for professional development in order for teachers and programs to maintain their certifications and licenses. In addition, every staff member deserves a professional development plan that is individualized to her needs and includes ongoing supervision, professional development and training, and evaluation for continuing growth (see Chapter 7 for more on this). NAEYC (2017) recommends that programs develop a program-wide professional development plan (PPDP) that sets intentional goals for professional competencies across the program and works reciprocally with individual professional development plans.

Health

Every center is required to have a health plan that meets certain criteria. For example, a licensed early childhood education program is required to have medical information on each child on file. This file may include proof of an annual physical examination, up-to-date immunization records, allergies,

and medications. In some states, staff members also need to have an annual physical and a doctor's confirmation that they are free of communicable diseases. States also require specific protocol and plans for maintaining a healthy program environment, such as what to do when a child becomes ill, procedures for administering medication, managing infectious disease control, and injury prevention measures.

Contact your local and state licensing agencies to obtain complete guidelines and regulations applicable to your specific program early on in the licensing process, and keep their contact information as well as their websites handy. Sign up to receive any online notifications and to keep informed of any updates or changes in regulation.

The Licensing Process

While it can feel overwhelming at first, there are ways to break down the process of obtaining a program license so it feels more feasible. Ensuring that your program space, staff, materials, and curriculum meet regulation standards is not something that can be rushed. Give yourself plenty of time to organize and prepare the various aspects of your program for inspection. As previously mentioned, you will need to familiarize yourself with local and state regulations. All states have an agency responsible for overseeing early childhood education and care, though the name of the agency varies by state. Licensing policies and forms can be found online and should be reviewed and filled out very carefully. Printing out the entire regulation book is worthwhile so that you can walk around your center and check off all the requirements line by line, ensuring that everything has been covered.

At the same time, you should also understand your local bylaws or rules regarding your program license. For example, some cities have certain quiet hours that should be noted when planning for outdoor play or other program community events. Others have rules regarding traffic patterns that might impact the program's schedule for drop-off and pickup. Get to know your local building inspectors and their regulations. Start at your local town hall and ask the building department where to begin.

Once you obtain your initial license to operate your program, you will need to renew it every few years. If you view keeping up with standards and requirements as an ongoing process, the renewal will be a much smoother path. Schedule a specific time each year to review any new or updated regulations that may have occurred since your last license renewal, and update the policies and procedures outlined in your family and staff handbooks to reflect these changes.

Partnering with Your Licensor

Going through the licensing process can be intimidating, but building a relationship with your licensor from the beginning can help ease your anxiety. If possible, obtain the name of your licensor and reach out to introduce yourself and let that person know that you're looking forward to working with her to improve your program. By developing a relationship with your licensor, you will

> Become more comfortable asking questions about regulations and the process as well as inquiring if the licensor has any helpful advice

> Better understand the licensor's perspective—and, in turn, help the licensor understand the philosophies that inform your program's views and practices

> See the licensor as a colleague and partner to help you meet your program's goals rather than as an obstacle or barrier

Knowing how to creatively and competently compromise is a helpful skill to hone. Imagine that your licensor takes issue with the amount of paper—photos, artwork, writing samples— fixed to classroom and hallway walls, citing it as a fire hazard. Your program's teachers, on the other hand, strongly believe that it is important to showcase the children's work, and they object to removing the paper. Is there any middle ground between the requirement and maintaining this component of your program's best practices? After some thought, you could decide to cut back on the volume of work displayed at one time, using documentation space more intentionally and putting more work in children's portfolios.

Directly from a Director

Often, I found licensing regulations fragmented or unclear. It is helpful to talk with a friend, colleague, or someone who has been through the process to help guide you. Preparing for licensing and going through the process helped me put many different elements of the program, including administrative decisions regarding safety, curriculum, and professional development of the teachers, into a more logical, systematic mental image, almost like a cognitive map.

Accreditation

Researchers have documented the positive outcomes of high-quality early childhood education, including readiness for school, greater academic achievement, higher rates of school completion, lower rates of incarceration, and higher incomes (NRC 2000). Studies also show that improving the quality of early childhood education programs can be achieved through systems building, such as by seeking national accreditation (Gerber, Whitebrook, &

Directly from a Director

When I realized how nervous my staff was about the upcoming accreditation site visit, I decided to plan a mock visit so we could get a feel for what it would actually be like. I let teachers know in advance that I would be asking a colleague from another center to come and observe some classrooms the following week. During her observation, she used the checklists and templates our accreditor would use. At the end of the week, she attended our staff meeting to share her observations and feedback. The teachers were pleased by the positive feedback she noted and found her constructive feedback on areas that needed improvement helpful. The exercise made everyone feel more prepared and at ease for the actual site visit.

Weinstein 2007; McDonald 2009; NYCECPDI 2009) or participating in a state quality rating and improvement system (QRIS).

Whereas program licensure indicates only that your program meets minimum standards for care, the best indicator of quality early care and education is accreditation. *Accreditation* is a voluntary process designed to measure, evaluate, and improve programs in a number of areas, including curriculum, teaching approaches, and family engagement. Accrediting bodies require programs to achieve and maintain standards that exceed the local and state regulatory requirements. Many accreditation processes involve extensive self-study as well as validation by professionals outside the program to verify that set standards of excellence are met.

While this process involves a significant amount of time and cost, experienced program leaders and staff find the accreditation process valuable and well worth it. The self-study portion offers the opportunity for self-reflection as a community as well as a helpful way to identify the program's strengths and areas for improvement. Families often appreciate having input into the process as well, and their participation gives them a better understanding of accreditation as a measure of quality. A further benefit of accreditation is that it marks your program as high quality, which can help you attract both new families and well-qualified staff.

In the United States, there are several national organizations that accredit early childhood programs, including the National Association for the Education of Young Children (NAEYC, NAEYC.org); National Association for Family Child Care (NAFCC, www.nafcc.org); National Early Childhood Program Accreditation (NECPA, www.necpa.net), and Council on Accreditation (COA, www.coanet.org).

NAEYC Accreditation of Early Learning Programs

The NAEYC Accreditation process is tailored to each program, so the path for implementation looks different for everyone. In general, the process follows four steps.

Step 1 — Enrollment

Begin by completing and submitting an enrollment form. Using the self-study materials provided by NAEYC, learn more about the accreditation standards and best practices, gather information about your program, and determine its strengths and challenges. As needed, develop and implement improvements, evaluate the results, and determine next steps. Carefully document all data and progress.

Step 2 — Application and Eligibility

After enrollment, you must determine and demonstrate that your program meets the eligibility requirements to become an applicant for accreditation. Part of this step includes building on the reflective work of your self-study to proceed to self-assessment. The self-assessment is formal and improvement focused, and it involves collecting observable and portfolio evidence that demonstrates how your program meets the NAEYC Early Learning Program Accreditation Standards:

> Relationships

> Curriculum

> Teaching

> Assessment of Child Progress

> Health

> Staff Competencies, Preparation, and Support

> Families

> Community Relationships

> Physical Environment

> Leadership and Management

Step 3 — Candidacy

Submit candidacy materials that prove, among other things, your program's satisfactory performance in meeting the NAEYC Early Learning Program Accreditation Standards and preparedness for a site visit.

Step 4 — Accreditation Site Visit

An NAEYC assessor visits the program to complete an independent assessment and collect data for scoring. The assessor randomly selects at least half of the program's classes (to a maximum of 10) to observe. This is your opportunity to provide the portfolio evidence compiled throughout previous steps to demonstrate how you and your staff are meeting the NAEYC Early Learning Program Accreditation Standards.

To learn more about NAEYC Accreditation of Early Learning Programs, visit NAEYC.org/accreditation/early-learning-program-accreditation.

Quality Rating Improvement Systems

The disparity in the demands between meeting licensing requirements and achieving national accreditation is often significant. A quality rating and improvement system (QRIS) is a tool developed by individual states that can help identify and bridge the gap between basic regulatory requirements and rigorous accreditation standards. *QRIS* is a "systemic approach to assess, improve, and communicate the level of quality in early and school-age care and education programs" (NCECQA 2018). It first came about in the 1990s when state governments saw a need for early childhood care and education programs to have consistent, clearly defined steps that aligned statewide in order to progress from meeting licensing standards to reaching accreditation standards (NCECQA 2018). As a program achieves each of these successive steps, it receives a higher quality rating that not only reflects the improvements made but also makes the program more attractive to families looking for a high-quality educational setting for their children.

While some states do not require programs to participate in the state's QRIS, in other states it is mandatory for programs receiving public funds (National Center on Child Care Quality Improvement 2015). There are often financial incentives to get involved with QRIS, as well as technical assistance, which vary from state to state. As of January 2017, the United States has 49 states, plus the District of Columbia and five territories, that are planning for, piloting, or implementing QRIS either regionally or statewide (QRIS NLN 2017).

The Flow of the Year: A Director's Big-Picture To-Do List

It's easy to get deeply involved in the details of each busy day, week, or month, but as director, you must always keep in mind what needs to be done over the course of the year—the big picture. Your plate is packed with everything from enrollment to finances, from hiring staff to attending board meetings. Maintaining a broad to-do list with larger tasks and deadlines broken out by month over the course of the school year can help keep you organized and ensure that your program transitions smoothly through each cycle of the year.

On the next two pages is a sample to-do list you might maintain to visualize your responsibilities over a 12-month period. Of course, every program is unique, with its own operation schedule, requirements, deadlines, obligations, and activities, but this is an example of the kinds of long-term projects that are helpful to track this way.

Twelve-Month Big-Picture To-Do List for a September-to-August Program Director

September
> First day of new year
> Plan for fall staff professional development day

October
> Organize classroom curriculum nights
> Create preliminary draft of the next fiscal year's budget
> Begin next year's enrollment process
> Hold fall family get-together

November
> Hold fall staff professional development day
> Hold open house for prospective families

December
> Conduct family conferences and share progress reports
> Finalize tuition schedule for next year's enrollment and reenrollment packets
> Submit NAEYC accreditation annual report and fee
> Plan for spring professional development day

January
> Order supplies and equipment
> Begin reenrollment process
> Hold professional development day for all staff
> Conduct midyear individual staff progress and goal adjustment meetings

February
> Hold spring staff professional development day
> Make end-of-year budget projections

March
> Finalize enrollment contracts
> Begin search to fill expected staff openings and hiring process for known openings for the coming year

April
> Set school calendar for next year

May
> Conduct family conferences and share progress reports
> Hold spring family get-together

Twelve-Month Big-Picture To-Do List for a September-to-August Program Director (continued)

June
- Hold end-of-school-year activities
- Send out annual family survey
- Conduct annual performance evaluations for all staff
- Order supplies and equipment

July
- Prepare monthly tuition bills for the new school year, which begins in September
- Finalize calendars for staff meetings and family meetings
- Review current licensing regulations and update policies and procedures
- Create and update your director 12-month big-picture to-do list for the next school year

August
- Prepare and deliver updated staff handbooks
- Send out annual family welcome/welcome back packet
- Prepare payroll for coming year
- Schedule classroom observations and ongoing staff supervision meetings for the coming year
- Hold meetings with individual teachers to finalize goals for the coming year
- Work with family board chairs to plan the event calendar for the year (e.g., social, educational, and fundraising events)
- Hold orientation for incoming staff
- Conduct mandatory training and review of policies and procedures for new and returning staff
- Hold intake meetings with new families and teachers
- Host summer classroom visits for new children and families
- Host new classroom and new teacher visits for children transitioning to new classrooms in the fall
- Hold classroom summer picnics to meet new staff and families
- Have teacher preparation week for cleaning and setting up classrooms

While this chapter provides a broad overview of developing policies and procedures and undergoing licensing and accreditation processes, we hope it has provided you with a starting point. When undertaken collaboratively with staff, families, and colleagues, these processes build consensus and community. Don't be afraid to ask questions and seek support from peers and more seasoned directors or professionals. Establish a network of local directors and reach out to talk about policy making or the accreditation or licensing process— or any shared experience—to receive advice and gain the confidence you need to grow in your role.

Big-Picture Takeaways

> Policies and procedures provide a transparent framework of program guidelines and expectations for staff and families.

> Licensure is necessary for the legal operation of a center; regulations vary from state to state, and there are local rules to also be accounted for.

> View your licensor and accreditor as your allies. They can help you understand and implement regulations and standards that ultimately improve the quality of your program.

Go Deeper

High-Quality Early Childhood Programs: The What, Why, and How, by L.J. Colker and D. Koralek (Redleaf Press, 2018)

Opportunities Exchange: http://opportunities-exchange.org

QRIS Resource Guide: https://qrisguide.acf.hhs.gov/index.cfm?do=qrisstate

Quality Compendium: https://qualitycompendium.org/view-state-profiles

The Visionary Director: A Handbook for Dreaming, Organizing, and Improvising in Your Center, Second Edition, by M. Carter and D. Curtis (Redleaf Press, 2010)

Chapter Four

Budget and Finances

A budget is telling your money
where to go instead of wondering
where it went.

—**John C. Maxwell,** as quoted in *The Total Money Makeover:
A Proven Plan for Financial Fitness*, by Dave Ramsey

Many early childhood directors find managing their program's budget the most challenging and least enjoyable part of their job. Most have been trained as teachers, not as finance or business professionals. If your program is large enough, you may have a business manager who oversees budgeting and finances; otherwise, this probably is your responsibility. To successfully run an early childhood program, you need to be organized, have some introductory bookkeeping and accounting knowledge, and have a structure in place, which may include some simple accounting software. This chapter focuses on working with an existing budget system; it clarifies some basic budget concepts and provides a few tips and strategies to make the best use of your budget.

Basic Budgeting Concepts

A budget is a tool for both short- and long-term finance planning to allocate money to the specific areas of your program's operations. Budget analysis helps you target your sources of revenue (income) to be sure you have money to meet your expenses. It also guides your fundraising efforts. To form an accurate picture of your program's financial situation, it is useful to begin with an analysis of the previous three years' budgets. Here are some questions to consider:

> What worked well in each of those years, and what did not work so well?

> Does the program have a manageable amount of debt? What are the monthly costs? Is there enough income to cover those costs plus a little more to grow your business? What interest rates are being paid?

> Has enrollment declined? If yes, does there seem to be a pattern?

> Is there a particular area of overspending?

> Does the tuition rate cover the full cost of care (to the extent possible)?

The answers to these questions will help you develop informed, realistic financial goals.

Identifying Revenue and Expenses

Just like your personal home budget, you need to know what money is coming in and what money is going out; in other words, what is your revenue and what are your expenses? The figure on the next page lists typical sources of revenue and types of expenses for early childhood programs. Some expenses, like rent and insurance, are fixed, while others (supplies, food) are variable. Variable costs fluctuate depending on a range of factors, including the number of children enrolled, the number of classrooms, and the number of teachers.

Typical Revenue Sources and Expenses for Early Childhood Programs

Revenue

> Registration fees
> Tuition
  - Parent fees
  - Subsidies
  - Scholarships
  - Reimbursements from school districts
  - Other outside sources
> Donations/fundraising
> Grants
> Child and Adult Care Food Program (CACFP) reimbursement

Expenses

> Staffing (salaries and benefits, staff professional development, consultants, substitutes)
> Building costs (rent, utilities) and facilities (janitorial, maintenance)
> Insurance (building, liability)
> Supplies (classroom, general office, kitchen)
> Learning materials and equipment (books, computers)
> Food
> Licensing and accreditation fees
> Marketing and advertising
> Transportation

Set up your budget in manageable segments of time, such as monthly, so you can easily compare projected and actual revenue and expenses. This will help you keep track of how you are doing fiscally and ensure that you have adequate cash flow. If you have large purchases one month, such as at the beginning of the school year, you will be aware that you must spend less in succeeding months to keep within the budget.

Developing Financial Policies and Procedures

Having clear, practical financial policies and procedures in place establishes protocols, standards, and expectations for money management; clarifies roles and responsibilities; and reinforces accountability. For example, what is the staff pay period schedule? Where are the financial records maintained and for how long? How do you ensure that financial records are kept confidential? Do you charge a penalty when families are late in making tuition payments? What other fees might families be charged? Address each of these points, and others relevant to your situation, in your program's policies and procedures and make them available to staff and families through vehicles such as the program handbooks.

Selecting a Financial Management System

There are two basic ways to keep track of your financial information: using an electronic spreadsheet system (like Microsoft Excel) or a budgeting software package (like QuickBooks, Procare Software, EZCare Childcare Management Software, or Brightwheel). Determining the best system for your needs depends on a number of factors:

> What are your needs? Are you looking for a system that manages just the budgeting and financial aspects of your program? Or do you require a comprehensive data management system that also tracks other information, such as attendance, child and staff records, and tuition collection?

> Who manages, or will manage, the business aspects of the program, and what is their expertise?

> How large or small an operation is the program?

> What technology and system do you currently own and use?

> Do you need (and do you have the resources for) a consultant to design a system for your particular needs?

> What kind of training and support are provided with the system you purchase?

Whatever system you use should be kept up to date on a weekly or monthly basis so you know the status of your finances in real time. Balancing the budget is a continuous process, not something that happens only at the end of the fiscal year. One way to closely monitor your program's financial health is with monthly reports. By keeping records of the program's financial activity current and readily available, you can use the information to prepare a fiscal report that will help you identify when and where revenue has decreased or if overspending is an issue (Neugebauer 2008).

Keeping your records up to date will also facilitate your quarterly, semiannual, or annual fiscal reporting. A typical fiscal report provides a spreadsheet with the income and expenses reconciled, as well as a narrative of any unusual circumstances during the period that may have impacted the budget (e.g., extra revenue due to a successful fundraiser, unusual expenses due to an unanticipated replacement of a major kitchen appliance). Review and discuss this information with your program's board of directors—and your direct supervisor, should you have one—to keep them apprised of the program's financial health and inform future budgetary approval decisions. You may also be required to file a fiscal report with your licensing agency, though it may not be reviewed in detail unless there is a problem.

Directly from a Director

When I started as a new director, the center's budget was a mess and in the red. No one really knew what the problem was because there wasn't a good record-keeping system. I decided we would track all expenses and income carefully for the next year. I announced this to all the staff and said everything would need to be accounted for with receipts. I was very surprised at the end of the year—we were in the black. Simply keeping track of where our money was going helped reduce unnecessary purchases.

It is helpful to have an outside independent review of your finances by an accountant on an annual basis. A certified public accountant (CPA) can also act in the role of financial advisor and provide important input to help you make critical financial decisions, such as expansion of the program, a remodeling construction project, or how to make up for loss of revenue due to low enrollment.

Tips and Strategies for Preparing an Effective Budget

Be Transparent and Assume Accountability

While many directors control their program's finances, it is important to include all stakeholders in the budgeting process in some capacity. Your staff is your most important resource. They have the insider perspective on priorities in the classroom and practical insights to share. If expenses need to be reduced, ask teachers for their input on what would have the least impact on their work. If you have a surplus at the end of the year, solicit their suggestions for how to use it. Even when you know you have very little to spend beyond the basic necessities, keeping the process and situation transparent will, in the long run, provide you with more support for difficult budget decisions. Other ways to be more transparent with your staff and families include sharing revenue and fundraising goals at the beginning of the fiscal year and providing quarterly updates about the budget at staff meetings.

Allow for Autonomy

If possible, give classroom teachers control over a small amount of money that can be used to enhance the curriculum at their discretion. For example, in the budget, allocate $200 a year to each teacher to purchase materials for a special project, arrange a field trip, or expand their classroom library. While some guidelines should be provided, it's important to allow teachers as much freedom as possible to decide how to use these funds. The amount of money is secondary to the message it conveys—that you trust your teachers to spend money wisely. You will find this goes a long way toward facilitating reciprocal trust and collaboration.

Be Strategic

Your budget tells a story, illustrating what is important to you and your program. For example, hiring and retaining quality staff is key to a successful organization, and the biggest chunk of a budget typically goes toward staff salaries and benefits. To attract well-qualified teachers, you'll need to not only budget competitive salaries but also consider other incentives: Do you provide health insurance and/or a retirement plan? Can you offer paid holidays or sick time? Are you able to allocate funds for staff to attend conferences or participate in other professional development opportunities? These benefits can be a significant or a relatively modest part of your program budget; for example, you may pay all or some of the cost of employees' health insurance, and you may set up and manage a retirement plan for staff to which the program makes contributions, or not.

With careful monitoring of the expenses and budget, you may find you have a surplus in some years. While you can seek input from staff on uses for surplus funds, as previously mentioned, a surplus can also become a source of discretionary funds (those not earmarked for essential expenses) that you use to further initiatives or improvements that tie into the center's vision and mission. Let's look at some examples of how the program's vision, mission, and initiatives could impact the way you use surplus funds or decide to raise discretionary funds:

Directly from a Director

Start your budget with the end in mind. Establish goals for the year and the resources you need to achieve them, and build your budget from there.

> If your center has high staff turnover and you find that your salaries are not competitive with those of other early childhood programs in the area, you may need to increase the money you spend on salaries to attract and retain quality teachers.

> If serving a diverse population is part of your program's mission, dedicate money for outreach initiatives.

> If developing healthy nutrition habits for children and families is a goal, prioritizing funds for healthy snacks and family education will be important.

> If family literacy is part of the needs of your population, dedicate funds for each classroom to have a rotating take-home backpack of children's books.

> If your program mission includes outdoor education, targeting funds for enhancing outdoor learning environments may be a fundraising goal.

> If you want to offer more support for children's social and emotional development, provide each classroom with funds to purchase children's books that address this theme.

> If you want to encourage more family engagement in your center, you might dedicate funds to coordinate more robust program community events.

Directly from a Director

Whenever possible, budget for a rainy-day fund and don't spend that money until there is no other way to proceed. Having a safety net in place makes tight times less stressful and more manageable.

Be Flexible

Build flexibility into your budget to meet unexpected expenses that may occur over the course of the year—a toilet that suddenly needs replacing or specialized materials for a newly enrolled child with a disability. This can be accomplished by having a discretionary budget line that is used for unexpected occurrences at the discretion of the director. If at the end of the year you have not used all of the discretionary funds and they cannot be carried over to the next year, you can always use them to purchase something in advance for the following year.

Help! What Do I Do When My Budget Isn't Working?

Sometimes you can plan your budget down to the last item and think you've anticipated every possible scenario, yet still discover some strategy or process is broken or ineffective in practice. In these cases, you need to act fast and do some damage control.

Step 1: Find Out What's Wrong

Discovering the root cause of the problem is the first step in solving it. Take time to review your budget and analyze what is happening. If you monitor your cash flow on a weekly or monthly basis, this should help you pinpoint the problem. Have expenses risen, revenue decreased, or both? Is this a one-time financial crisis or an ongoing issue, such as enrollment declining over a period of time?

Step 2: Reduce Your Expenses

Your next countermeasure is to decrease the amount of money going out.

> **Manage staff hours.** Because staff payroll costs are the biggest part of every program budget, this is the most important way to reduce expenses. Make every effort to avoid having staff work overtime. If you don't have fixed arrival and departure times, determine exactly when and how many children arrive and leave in each class so you do not overstaff classrooms early and late in the day.

> **Prioritize your purchases.** Identify which items are necessary and which are optional. What can be delayed until the program is in a more stable financial position, and what can be cut entirely?

> **Stretch your dollars.** This often requires some creative thinking. For example, does your program have a partner organization to split costs with, such as sharing substitutes across centers?

> **Get dividends on professional development.** Your professional development investment is not limited to the staff you are able to send to conferences or workshops. Send fewer teachers to these events, with the expectation that they will share what they have learned with the rest of the staff when they return.

Step 3: Speed the Inflow of Revenue

Collecting income more quickly can also help compensate for a period of lower-than-expected profits or higher-than-expected expenses.

> **Invoice promptly.** Issue invoices as quickly as possible to reinforce timely (or early) payment.

> **Offer incentives for early payers.** Consider enacting a bonus policy for payments that are made early, such as a 5 percent discount for bills paid in two lump installments over the year rather than monthly.

> **Penalize late payers.** To encourage families to pay on time, charge a fee for payments that are late and follow up promptly with overdue accounts.

Directly from a Director

Sometimes, keeping things simple is best. Our center realized we were regularly overspending what was budgeted for classroom materials. The teachers and I brainstormed and decided to inventory the materials we already had available in the center before making any more purchases. We worked hard to clean out teacher closets and storage rooms and really organize our materials. It was exciting to see missing toy pieces rediscovered and materials being traded across classrooms. In the end, the teachers were happy and we did not overspend what was budgeted for materials because there were fewer materials to purchase.

Step 4: Explore New Income Sources

When cutting costs and collecting anticipated income more quickly isn't enough, it is time to consider other ways to supplement the program's revenue. Exploring new income sources may require investment of some funds in the short term with the hope that you will raise more revenue in the long term. Before implementing any strategy, consider whether the increased potential for income outweighs any increased expenses.

> **Raise tuition fees.** This strategy might be something to consider implementing universally or more selectively, such as for families who enroll their children after a certain date.

> **Boost enrollment.** Do targeted outreach. For example, if the Farsi-speaking population of your community is a relatively untapped market, you might have your program's marketing collateral and website translated into Farsi. (See Chapter 9 for more information on this strategy.)

> **Expand the program.** Add or offer new services, such as an early morning drop-off, an after-school component, accepting more children in certain classrooms, or opening a new center branch.

> **One-shot appeals.** Write an appeal letter to alumni families, former staff, board members, and other stakeholders with a request for donations, noting why tuition fees do not cover the full costs of running a quality program and outlining ways additional funds would improve children's learning opportunities.

> **Ongoing activities with a separate fee.** Offer additional activities for families and others in the community, such as parenting seminars, weekend activities, or computer classes, for a fee.

> **Rent out space after hours.** Offer your space for a fee to community groups, such as book clubs or support or scouting groups.

> **Grants.** Apply for relevant local and foundation grants or public funding.

Keys to Successful Fundraising

Fundraising can be an invaluable supplement to a tight program budget. Planning is key to any successful fundraising endeavor, and there are a number of things to consider:

> **Demographics of the program community.** Carefully consider who your fundraiser will be aimed at. Events that draw in others from the community can help supplement what families are able to contribute. Also, provide a variety of ways for families to participate in a fundraising event so they can choose to contribute in ways they feel comfortable with, such as donating their time and skills rather than funds.

> **Someone to take charge.** Organize a team of volunteers to form a fundraising committee, making sure to include both families and staff members to support your family and community engagement efforts. Ask a few key family members to help, and make sure teachers support the project. Enthusiasm from you and the staff will carry over to the families. Without support from families and staff, any idea, no matter how good it is, may not be successful.

FUNdraising Ideas

Spare change collection jars

Have children decorate mason jars, shoeboxes, or small clay flowerpots. Post them by the classroom doors for families and visitors to drop in their spare change.

Car wash

Hold a "pay-what-you-can" car wash one weekend in the center's parking lot.

Silent auction

Ask families, community members, and local businesses to donate items and services to be part of an auction at a school event.

Raffles

Should your local and state laws allow it, a raffle is another great option. As with the silent auction, ask for prize items and services to be donated by the community. Sell tickets, priced so everyone can participate, and hold the drawing during a center-wide get-together, such as an end-of-the-year party.

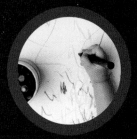

Repurpose and sell children's artwork

After obtaining permission from the children's families, collect drawings and other artwork created by children in the program and reproduce them to sell as personalized stationery.

Benefit nights

Collaborate with a local or national restaurant, organizing an event where the school community gathers and brings business to the restaurant, earning a portion of the proceeds in exchange. Check into a similar arrangement with a food truck that can come to the center.

> **Purpose and goals.** Know why you are holding a fundraiser and communicate this to everyone involved and to potential supporters. Targeted fundraising with a specific purpose and amount to raise is more successful than fundraising efforts to support the center in general. For example, you might decide to raise $1,000 to purchase new playground equipment or for children to take field trips. Tie the fundraising goals to the children's learning and well-being, emphasizing how they will benefit.

> **Frequency.** Having too many events will dilute both efforts and interest, and you risk burning out or even alienating families and the community—your core donors. Instead, focus on planning a few select events to yield more funds and be more efficient.

> **Timing.** Put your fundraising events on the calendar early and choose your approach and dates strategically. For example, an event like a community yard sale with proceeds to benefit the center will be better attended and more successful in warm weather.

> **Education value.** How does your fundraiser align with your program's mission or philosophy? If you are selling a product, articulate how that relates to the center's educational goals. For example, you might host a children's book fair where your program receives a percentage of the sales; the goal could be to use the money raised to purchase audiobooks in different languages to support the linguistic diversity in your center.

> **Communication.** Keeping families and the community involved and informed about the progress of an ongoing fundraiser is key to keeping momentum and motivation going. Have a kickoff event that communicates your goals—how much money you want to raise and how it will be used. Keep the community updated on how much money is raised each week through newsletters, emails, message boards, and meetings. When the event is over, share the total amount raised and remember to thank people enthusiastically for their help and participation.

While this chapter focuses on the basics for managing an existing budget, many of the principles discussed are the same for designing a budget from scratch. Begin by identifying your streams of revenue (tuition being the largest revenue source) and your expenses (staff salaries and benefits being the largest expense). You will also need to include startup costs, which are often underestimated even though they include large, critical expenses like furniture, equipment and materials, and remodeling. Build in a financial cushion or safety net to help you through the initial six months while your enrollment grows. Any good business plan needs to be detailed and comprehensive before approaching business partners or lenders.

Big-Picture Takeaways

> Establish a baseline for your program's financial health. Begin by analyzing the previous three years' budget and determining what's working and what isn't.

> Monitor your budget on a weekly or monthly basis. This will allow you to see patterns, notice irregularities, and implement new strategies before small problems become big headaches.

> Be strategic. Establish your goals and the resources you need to get there, but allow for flexibility to manage financial hiccups as they arise.

Go Deeper

The Art of Leadership: Managing Money in Early Childhood Organizations, edited by R. Neugebauer (Exchange Press, 2017)

The Business of Child Care: Management and Financial Strategies, by G. Jack (Cengage, 2005)

US Small Business Administration (SBA): www.sba.gov

Chapter Five

>> Program Curriculum

Education . . . is a process of living and
not a preparation for future living.

—John Dewey, *My Pedagogic Creed*

Curriculum is at the core of every educator's work, and research proves the importance of high-quality early learning experiences for children (see Camilli et al. 2010; Jordan et al. 2014; Yoshikawa et al. 2013). In some programs, decisions about curriculum may be handled by a board or committee that is part of the sponsoring organization, and the director's input into the selection or development process varies. In other cases, the director is responsible for overseeing how curriculum is developed and implemented. Whatever your situation is, you are responsible wholly or in part for

> Establishing your program's educational framework and guidelines

> Making sure your program implements a curriculum that is developmentally appropriate, is consistent with its goals, and is responsive to the population you serve

> Leading teachers in integrating best practices with early learning standards

A curriculum "provides a blueprint for planning and implementing a program"—in other words, deciding what to teach and how (Dodge 2004). Having a strong, comprehensive, and well-implemented curriculum helps attract families, engage children and support their learning, and fulfill teachers. As Frede and Ackerman note, "The quality and content of the curriculum . . . will influence the effectiveness of any preschool program" (2007, 12). With a curriculum that aptly fits your program in place, you and your staff can make decisions about what and how to teach so your program realizes its goal of enhancing children's knowledge and skills (Dodge 2004; Frede & Ackerman 2007).

Directly from a Director

A good program needs both pedagogical *and* administrative leadership.

How Do You Decide the Best Curriculum Approach or Model for Your Program?

High-quality early childhood programs develop or adopt a comprehensive, developmentally appropriate curriculum that addresses all domains of children's development as well as the content disciplines that provide a foundation for later learning:

> Physical development (fine and gross motor skills)

> Social and emotional development

> Cognitive development

> Language and literacy development

> Creativity and the arts

> Mathematics, science, and technology

> Social studies

From these fundamental tenets, curriculum development depends on the program's setup and can be approached in many ways. While individual classroom teachers should have some independence in their classrooms, the overarching philosophy and curriculum guide the program as a whole.

Before making any decisions about an appropriate curriculum approach or model, Dodge (2004) suggests examining your specific program's

> **Mission and/or vision statements.** How can the curriculum reflect the goals and values of your program?

> **Philosophical beliefs.** How do children learn best? How are children's needs best supported? What is the role of teachers in instruction? How does your program support and engage families?

> **Mandates and requirements.** Is your program required to adopt a specific curriculum model or approach in order to be part of a state-funded initiative? What other regulations do you need to consider when developing or adopting a curriculum?

> **Teachers.** What supports will teachers need to develop and implement a meaningful curriculum? How much guidance will they need?

> **Available time for staff development.** How much time will you and teachers need to discuss and plan curriculum? Is it feasible?

> **Available resources to support curriculum implementation.** Will teachers need extensive training, and will your budget cover those expenses? Which materials and equipment does your program already have, and which will need to be purchased?

The answers to these questions provide you with the parameters, information, and direction needed to guide you in making decisions about the program's curriculum. Certain considerations will carry more weight depending on the program. By carefully considering these features of your program's landscape, you can select or develop and implement a curriculum that is intentional and successful.

As you consider a particular curriculum framework or a specific model that you believe will fit your program best, critically reflect on the following with teachers and, as appropriate, the families of the children you serve:

> Does the curriculum align with your program's values and goals? (Dodge 2004)

> Is the curriculum developmentally appropriate?

> Is the curriculum based on current research? (Dodge 2004)

> Does the curriculum integrate learning domains, or are they addressed separately? (Frede & Ackerman 2007)

> Is the curriculum easy to understand? (Dodge 2004)

> Is the curriculum flexible enough to accommodate the needs and abilities of individual children?

> Is the curriculum consistent with the culture of your community?

> If applicable, does the curriculum meet any local, state, or national requirements your program must abide by?

> Does the curriculum connect with your state's early learning standards?

> Does the curriculum comprehensively outline the basic information and guidance needed for teachers to implement it? (Dodge 2004)

> Is the curriculum proven to be effective? (Dodge 2004)

> Does the curriculum make use of the full scope of teachers' knowledge and skills?

> Are resources available to support staff in implementation? (Dodge 2004)

> Does the curriculum clearly address outcomes and expectations? How is children's learning assessed?

> Are there tools available to determine how well the curriculum is being implemented? (Dodge 2004)

> Does the curriculum involve families and strengthen the home–school partnership? (Frede & Ackerman 2007)

Often, discussing these questions will lead to meaningful conversations about program improvement and challenges that might be specific to the families you serve. Listen carefully to feedback and be open minded about adjustments to the curriculum framework. The more preparation done during the curriculum development process, the more successful the implementation will be.

Curriculum Approaches

While it is beyond the scope of this chapter to discuss the many different early childhood curriculum approaches and models and their underlying educational philosophies, this section provides an overview of a few types of curricula commonly used in early childhood programs.

Best practice supports the thoughtful, intentional use of both child- and adult-initiated experiences—children and adults share the responsibility for learning (Epstein 2014). Your curriculum should be in harmony with the way you believe children learn and the role you feel teachers play in that learning (Frede & Ackerman 2007). Are you looking for a curriculum that lays out instruction for teachers? Do you want a curriculum that gives them more freedom to design instruction and activities around the children's interests, needs, and characteristics? Does one type of approach described here appeal most to you, but others seem like they might offer something for your program as well? While the approaches

Directly from a Director

I am a director because I love children and education. I love watching children fall in love with learning. In this role, I have the pleasure of watching this magic unfold again and again across an entire school community.

discussed have been categorized in a way that makes their hallmarks as clear as possible, they are not necessarily exclusive of one another. For example, some commercially available curricula, such as Creative Curriculum Solutions and the HighScope Curriculum series, are grounded in a theoretical model that views children as instrumental in their own learning; these curricula are intended to be used in an environment rich with opportunities to explore through play with adult scaffolding and support. In practice, many programs weave together elements of more than one curriculum approach to fit the needs of the children, teachers, and families.

Packaged Curricula

Commercially available early childhood curricula vary widely in terms of the scope and depth of content, flexibility, the role of adults, how children participate in learning, and other factors. Some offer step-by-step, even scripted, lessons and activities to be taught in a specific way in a specific sequence; they may be largely standardized with content that is not driven by or responsive to children's interests, skills, and needs. Others provide more of a framework to guide teachers' interactions with children and help teachers develop activities that are tailored to the particular needs of the children they serve. Curricula meeting this description often provide ideas and opportunities to individualize or modify instructional practices. They also may be adaptable to other approaches, such as play-based learning and emergent curriculum.

Some programs are required to choose a packaged curriculum. In programs with more latitude, some directors prefer to use packaged curricula because they are designed for immediate implementation and are particularly helpful in supporting teachers with limited experience or educational background. Packaged curricula also provide a unified framework, often organized as subject-based or themed units that represent what is believed to be important for children to learn, with clearly defined expectations across different classrooms and ages. Many include learning materials and an assessment component. Packaged curricula's easy-to-understand format also makes the process of sharing children's learning with their families fairly straightforward. Using a curriculum developed by a respected organization in the education field instills confidence in the quality of the content. However, a packaged curriculum can be a high-cost investment—including training—and you will need to budget for its purchase.

When reviewing a packaged curriculum, carefully consider whether it provides a supportive structure for teaching and learning along with flexibility for teachers to adapt it to their particular group of children. You might use one of these curricula more as a framework and encourage teachers to incorporate elements of other approaches in their teaching. Professional development support, both initial and ongoing, is also critical to successful implementation of any curriculum, no matter the experience or background of your staff.

Play-Based Learning

Play provides a meaningful context for active, engaged learning. It contributes to children's physical, cognitive, and social and emotional development, from problem solving and creativity to self-regulation skills to the management of stress and other strong emotions (Power 2000). *Play-based learning* is a curriculum approach that views play as the way children make sense of their world and do some of their best learning as they make choices, take risks, make mistakes, explore new ideas, and just have *fun* (Mardell et al. 2016). Children have many opportunities throughout the day to choose materials and initiate their own activities.

In *guided play,* there is a focus on facilitating specific learning goals within the context of child-directed play. Teachers make intentional choices of materials and carefully orchestrate the environment (Bustamante, Hirsh-Pasek, & Golinkoff 2017; Hassinger-Das, Hirsh-Pasek, & Golinkoff 2017; Weisberg et al. 2016). Teachers also influence play-based learning through their own participation in children's play choices; they may introduce more materials that enhance, extend, or scaffold children's learning, and they prompt children toward the learning goals with open-ended questions and comments.

The creative opportunities of this approach require program directors to invest in open-ended materials that are inviting and provide many different play opportunities. Because of the flexibility of play-based learning and the many forms it can take, you might find that some teachers need your support to understand how to intentionally scaffold children's learning. Explaining children's learning gains and goals to families can also be more challenging with this approach, because the learning that occurs is often more observable (e.g., a child explaining why she thinks her actions will result in a particular outcome) than tangible (e.g., a sheet of paper on which the child has practiced writing several letters following a teacher's model). As with emergent curriculum and project-based learning (see the following discussions), documentation is an important part of this curriculum approach.

Emergent Curriculum

With many packaged curricula and to some extent in play-based approaches, the curriculum is based on predetermined themes (e.g., children learn about pumpkins and apples and falling leaves in October, regardless of the local climate). In other programs, the curriculum, including topics of study, is more responsive to a particular group of children's experiences. One such approach is known as *emergent curriculum*, in which teaching and learning develop from children's specific interests and ideas. It is grounded in the belief that children learn best when their natural curiosities are respected, explored, and guided by a teacher; in other words, it is child initiated and teacher facilitated (Forman & Fyfe 2012). The process starts when teacher observes an interest emerge in the children. From there, they frame the curriculum and provide scaffolding, materials, and opportunities for the children to explore and learn more about the topic. When the teacher feels that the emergent topic has run its course or the children begin to express interest in a new topic, the process begins again.

This approach requires a great deal of observation, documentation, and flexibility. Teachers also must be able to begin by meeting each child where she is developmentally and provide appropriate challenges to scaffold a more complex understanding. As the curriculum cannot be prepared in advance, more planning and preparation are required and can be more time intensive. There are times when planning emergent curriculum can feel overwhelming, but it often results in joyful, creative experiences for both the children and the teachers. No year is exactly the same, no strategy prescribed, and the feeling of ownership in the classroom can be extremely rewarding for teachers. Directors who want to cultivate an interest in pedagogy and an *inquiry stance*—an openness to questions and change—in teachers find the emergent curriculum approach a great fit for their program. Families also enjoy watching their children's interests bloom into developed knowledge. To support teachers in this process, you will need to provide access to a variety of open-ended materials and books.

Project-Based Learning

Project-based learning, also known as the *project approach,* is a curriculum strategy in which children actively explore real-world questions, challenges, and concepts through in-depth, hands-on investigations and research (Helm & Katz 2016). These investigations might be initiated by children or the teacher, and children can work in small groups, as part of the whole class, or even individually (Helm & Katz 2016). The approach has a complex but flexible framework that allows for different levels of experiences and exploration (Katz, Chard, & Kogan 2014).

The integration of learning and doing allows directors and teachers to create a loose curriculum framework and set learning goals that are informed more specifically based on children's interests throughout the year. As with emergent curriculum, project-based learning curriculum is current, based in children's curiosity, and can head in spontaneous and creative directions. Again, this means that teachers will need more time to plan and prepare in the short term. While project work can be easily individualized for children and is often deeply motivating for both teachers and children, it can be challenging to ensure that the investigative phases are complex enough for children and that they connect to different areas of early learning standards. Sharing what children are learning with families requires ongoing documentation of the project, which may include work samples, photographs, and transcripts of children's words, ideas, and questions. Documentation offers families a way to contribute their feedback and thoughts about the project. (For more on documentation, see Chapter 6.)

Curriculum guides the decisions you and your staff make about room arrangement, materials, interactions with children, and experiences that support learning and children's enjoyment of it. While you may not have complete control over the selection and implementation of your program's curriculum, you can look for ways to help teachers examine these aspects of their classrooms and identify ways to most effectively support their young learners.

In centers that follow an established educational approach, method, or model, the principles of the program's curriculum are already dictated. A brief overview of three prevalent early childhood education models can be found on page 74.

A Look at Some Influential Early Childhood Education Models

It is important to have a general understanding of a variety of early childhood education models and their hallmarks. Here are just a few. You can find more information and background on each through the website listed at the end of each description.

Montessori Method

This method gives each child the freedom to choose what they need to learn and develop at their own individual pace while supported by teacher instruction or modeling in technique, social behavior and interactions, and extending play experiences. There are five core components of a Montessori program: teachers trained in the method, multiage classrooms, use of Montessori materials, work that is child directed, and uninterrupted work periods for children to complete tasks at their own pace (American Montessori Society 2018). Educators set up the classroom environment to provide a wide range of specially designed materials that are organized into five learning areas—culture, language, mathematics, practical life, and sensorial. (www.montessori.edu)

Reggio Emilia Approach

This approach is based on the belief that children's natural development and relationships with others should guide their learning opportunities. Children direct their learning by exploring, observing, hypothesizing, tinkering, and expressing themselves. Educators scaffold these experiences to help children engage actively and more deeply with materials and topics. The importance of creating and fostering strong relationships with other children, families, teachers, and the community is also emphasized. (www.reggiochildren.it)

Waldorf Education

This model highlights the role of children's imagination in the learning process. It integrates academic, practical, and artistic development with the aim of inspiring children to be independent, enthusiastic, ethically responsible, lifelong learners, and it incorporates the arts in all academic disciplines to enhance and enrich learning. Educators create daily routines that include circle time, free indoor and outdoor play, artistic work, and practical tasks. Waldorf classrooms are designed to resemble a home environment. Materials and toys are made from natural materials to strengthen children's connection to nature; their simplicity encourages open-ended, creative play. (www.waldorfeducation.org)

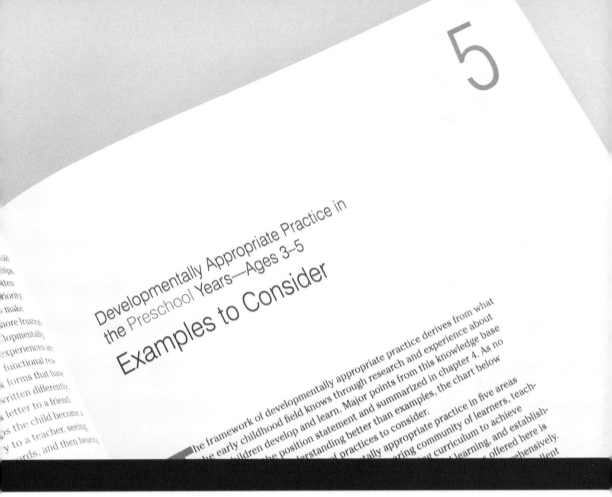

Developmentally Appropriate Practice in
the Preschool Years—Ages 3–5

Examples to Consider

Integrating Best Practices and Early Learning Standards

Early learning standards are statewide expectations outlining what children from birth to age 5 should know and be able to do at specific ages. All 56 US states and territories have developed standards for preschoolers, and almost all have developed standards for infants and toddlers (NCECQA 2017). Whatever curriculum approach or method your program uses, its learning goals for children should align with your state's standards. Remember that standards indicate *what* is taught but not *how* it is taught. They provide an understanding of what children should know and be able to do, but it is up to you to help teachers provide experiences to support children's development of the skills and knowledge they need. Use the standards to guide your development or selection of a curriculum, and work with the teachers on understanding the purpose of standards and how to use them as a framework to implement the curriculum. Dedicate portions of your staff meetings for teaching teams to share how they are implementing the learning standards in developmentally appropriate and responsive ways.

Supporting Your Teachers in Implementing Curriculum

After developing or selecting the right curriculum approach—or approaches!—for your program, your role is to guide and support teachers in the implementation process. You might create uniform lesson-planning templates for teachers to fill in and share with you on a regular basis, such as every week or every two weeks. Depending on the curriculum approach and your leadership style, a less formal process might be established, like periodic scheduled or impromptu meetings to discuss what teachers are planning and preparing. When implementing a curriculum that is new for the program, teachers may need more time, attention, and guidance from you. Once teachers are more experienced and comfortable, your involvement in the day-to-day lesson plans will likely be more limited to review and targeted feedback and modeling and supporting teachers' reflective practice.

Help teaching teams create a consistent (such as weekly or monthly) schedule to meet and prepare that coordinates with full staff meetings so they are prepared in advance to present and share their lesson plans. Since full staff meetings are often a time to assess how curriculum is moving along across the entire program rather than to address specific concerns, you might note any issues that arise during these meetings and then meet with specific teachers and teaching teams later to discuss these issues or concerns. If there is high staff turnover, take the time to make sure new teachers are trained to implement the curriculum. Plan on holding at least two staff trainings a year to keep everyone up to date in methods and strategies and to discuss experiences, feedback, and ideas for improving how the curriculum approach is implemented. You will also need to allocate resources—including funds, materials, equipment, and professional development—to support teachers in implementing the curriculum effectively and successfully.

Feeling engaged, well supported, and fulfilled in one's work is an important part of staff retention and morale (discussed in more detail in Chapter 7). Here are some ways you might support teachers as they plan and use the curriculum (Dodge 2004):

> Resources such as books, journals, and videos

> Observations in other classrooms

> Coaching and mentoring from other teachers or consultants

> Time for self-reflection and discussion

> Online trainings

When the Curriculum in Your Program Is Not Working

Quinn has just started as director of a program that has been in operation for more than 25 years. As part of her efforts to familiarize herself with the learning environment of the program, she sits in on a number of classrooms to observe. She's troubled by what she sees. Many of the children do not seem engaged or excited, and while teachers appear to notice this, they do not deviate from the curriculum manual.

After months of evaluation and gathering input from teachers and families, the program that Fatina directs has adopted and started to implement a new curriculum approach. Both Fatina and her staff are excited to be moving to this curriculum, but it quickly becomes clear that there is an unbalanced focus on developmental areas. While there is a heavy emphasis on cognitive development, the children's social and emotional skills are hardly addressed, with few opportunities for children to play together, solve problems, or pursue interesting topics in depth.

Both Quinn and Fatina find themselves asking the same question: "Now what?"

In each scenario explored here, the director feels the program's curriculum is dated or not working. This is not an uncommon situation.

Quinn's situation touches on something that directors across the country express: curriculum quality is heavily dependent on teachers' ability to implement it. Hiring qualified, passionate teachers (discussed in more depth in Chapter 7) and providing the curriculum framework is not the end of your work. It is equally important for you to give teachers both autonomy and oversight as they develop, adapt, and modify the curriculum for their classrooms. Effective teachers know their learners, and they need to recognize when following a curriculum verbatim isn't working and feel comfortable making adaptations for the group and for individual children. When teachers are given autonomy, they feel ownership over their classrooms and the curriculum development process, and they are less hesitant to make necessary modifications.

With this autonomy, there also needs to be director support, feedback, and guidance. During staff meetings and one-on-one meetings with teachers, ask them to share what is happening with the children and their curriculum

Directly from a Director

I tell my staff they can integrate parts of the curriculum with their own style. I want them to have some ownership of what they do in the classroom.

ideas. Ask questions and help them identify any problem areas. What are children excited about in the curriculum? Are the children focused and engaged with the activities? How do you know what they are learning? What are *your* goals and objectives for the children's learning? Are those goals both challenging and achievable? What do you think is working and not working with your curriculum? Less experienced teachers may need more guidance in developing effective, meaningful learning experiences for the children, including setting developmentally appropriate goals, identifying the types of questions they should ask to facilitate learning, individualizing teaching strategies to meet diverse needs, and documenting and assessing whether the objectives are met. While more experienced teachers may not need this level of support, they might need guidance in applying newer understandings in best practice or moving from a more directive curriculum approach that they have been used to and comfortable with to one in which adults and children share more of the responsibility for learning.

How Do Teachers Document Their Implementation of the Curriculum?

Your staff handbook should outline how teachers are expected to plan, record, implement, document, and assess the curriculum in their classrooms. Many regulations also require that lesson plans be posted for viewing as well as stored for inspection. It is best to have a single system in place for all classrooms to use. This will make it easier for you to review what is happening in the classrooms and provide feedback. You might require teachers to keep their weekly lesson plans and notes in a binder or file box in their individual classrooms. When you stop by to observe a classroom, you can also quickly access and review these plans. Alternately, you might create an electronic template for teachers to populate and submit to you via email each week, or have teachers bring their lesson plans to their supervision meeting with you to review and discuss their plans in person.

Provide guidelines for teachers about sharing with families what their children are doing and learning in the classroom, including the frequency and structure of this communication. Some programs require a uniform format, such as branded and designed e-newsletters, while other programs allow variation between classrooms. In either case, it is extremely helpful to provide print or electronic templates or examples for teachers to better understand your expectations. Some flexibility should be allowed to meet families' needs. For example, a family whose home language is not English may find emails containing photographs or a short video clip of their child dismantling and exploring the inner workings of an old computer keyboard with real tools more helpful in understanding the curriculum than a written learning story describing the same activity. If your curriculum is play based, some families may come to you or to their children's teachers with concerns about whether children are being adequately prepared for kindergarten; work with your staff to increase their effectiveness at communicating the value of your curriculum.

Ongoing Maintenance of a High-Quality Curriculum

A successful program requires not only careful contemplation about choosing a curriculum but also ongoing consideration of the quality of children's educational experiences. Here are a few ways you can build on and improve what you know about high-quality learning to continue to offer a program that supports children's development:

> **Observe other programs** that have a reputation for using developmentally appropriate practices to see implementation of different curricula in action. Many programs are open to having visitors come and see what they do. Build a good relationship with that circle of program directors; they will be excellent mentors when you experience challenges.

> **Invite close colleagues to observe your program** and provide feedback and suggestions on the curriculum. Be open to their input and implement change based on their feedback.

> **Attend conferences** at the national, state, or regional level to stay current on research and practices in early childhood education. Should your budget allow for it, cover conference attendance for some or all of your teachers as part of their professional development.

> **Draw on your relationships with your licensor and accreditor.** Ask them questions that show a desire to improve your program curriculum, such as what upcoming informational sessions or trainings they would recommend.

> **Develop and send out a survey** to families and staff asking for their feedback on the program's curriculum and their suggestions for what could be improved.

Selecting, developing, implementing, and maintaining a high-quality curriculum is an ongoing process, and it might take years of careful planning and shaping to build your program's identity to articulate exactly what kind of curriculum is best for your classrooms. Be engaged in and enthusiastic about your program's curriculum. Your excitement will be contagious to your staff and the rest of the school community. If you feel that your program's approach to teaching and learning is stale or just not working, it's time to make things dynamic and new again!

Big-Picture Takeaways

> As director, it is your responsibility to establish your program's educational framework and guidelines. Make sure your curriculum is consistent with your program's goals and meets children's needs while promoting their learning and development, and lead teachers in integrating best practices with early learning standards.

> There are many different curriculum models, resources, and approaches. Carefully consider and evaluate which approach— and it may be a combination of several—is the best fit for your program.

> Provide teachers with ongoing support and feedback as they plan and implement the curriculum in their classrooms. A balance of director guidance and teacher autonomy often makes for a rich environment where effective and joyful teaching and learning can flourish.

Go Deeper

Developmentally Appropriate Practice in Early Childhood Programs Serving Children from Birth Through Age 8, Third Edition, edited by C. Copple and S. Bredekamp (NAEYC, 2009)

Insights and Inspirations from Reggio Emilia: Stories of Teachers and Children from North America, edited by L. Gandini, S. Etheredge, and L. Hill (Davis Publications, 2009)

Learning Together with Young Children: A Curriculum Framework for Reflective Teachers, Second Edition, by D. Curtis and M. Carter (Redleaf Press, 2017)

Chapter Six

Observation, Assessment, and Documentation

Pay attention.
Be astonished.
Tell about it.

—Mary Oliver, *Red Bird*

Observation and Assessment

Observation and assessment are basic tools of a director's toolbox. Through observation and various types of assessments, you collect data that provides evidence of what is working or not working in your program and in the classroom. Using this information, you and the teachers can make informed decisions on improvement plans and goal setting. This chapter will look at program assessment and child assessment, as well as the role of documentation in your program. (See Chapter 7 for a discussion of teacher observation and evaluation.)

Directly from a Director

I know a high-quality program when I see it. When I walk in the classroom, it is humming, joyful, and industrious. Children are engaged with materials and each other. Teachers are also engaged— observing, interacting with children, and documenting.

Program Assessment

When you walk into a classroom, you notice the physical environment—how the room is arranged, what's on the walls, what materials and books are displayed and how. You see how children are interacting with each other and how the teacher is interacting with them. While these observations can often give you an idea of the program's quality, this is not enough. Good program evaluation tools help you articulate your goals for children, families, and staff and help you all work together to improve the quality of the program. Accomplishing this involves collecting data through many sources such as observation, interviews, and surveys, and analyzing that data. A thorough assessment process then uses action planning and goal setting to connect where your program is to where you want it to be. This process is not solely the director's responsibility; it should include all your constituencies—staff, families, board members, and other outside agencies when relevant.

Gathering and Analyzing Evidence

Directors gather and organize evidence on the effectiveness of their programs each year. Ideally, you want to collect both quantitative and qualitative data. *Quantitative data* involves characteristics that can be measured in numbers (e.g., how often the children are given the opportunity for outdoor play, how frequently teachers communicate with families about children's learning), while *qualitative data* involves qualities that describe attributes or properties (e.g., children's level of engagement in activities, teacher–child interactions, relationships between teachers and families). You can collect evidence for program evaluation throughout the year using assessment tools like these:

- Systematic classroom observations using criterion-based checklists and scales as well as published assessment tools and accreditation instruments
- Written observations of classrooms and centerwide interactions
- Feedback from your licensor, accreditor, and/or QRIS rater
- Staff and family surveys (see "Sample Open-Ended Survey Questions" on page 84)
- Focus groups and interviews with families and staff
- Other program and classroom documentation, such as class portfolios

Identify the criteria for the program assessment, such as health and safety, curriculum, equipment and materials, teacher–child interactions, and family engagement. Many directors will use the broad categories of criteria from their annual program assessment required for licensing, accreditation, or QRIS.

While the annual program assessment process may involve some of the same information sources as an outside assessment, every program has its own unique goals and issues. You may be monitoring, evaluating, and setting long-term goals—anything from decreased staff turnover to enriched outdoor learning environments to tracking statistics on how many accidents children have while at the center—that are quite specific and not necessarily considered by your licensor, accreditor, or QRIS rater. An annual program assessment is most meaningful when the program focuses on unique goals and challenges as well as general best practices.

Sample Open-Ended Survey Questions

For Staff

> What do you like best about our program?

> Identify one to three things about our program you would like to improve or change (e.g., frequency of staff meetings, process of curriculum review, outdated policies) and why.

> What do you feel works well at our program?

> What supports or resources would help you do your job better?

For Families

> What do you like best about the program?

> What about the center would you like to see improved and how?

> What additional program services and activities would meet the needs of you and your child?

> Please share any other comments, questions, or feedback you would like to share with us about the quality of the program provided for you and your child.

To obtain more targeted information from staff and families, consider reworking some or all of these questions as multiple-choice items (adding specific, limited choices for each) or Likert-scale items.

You must also decide how the evidence will be collected. Some programs use informal assessments or published instruments exclusively. Others might include online survey tools like SurveyMonkey or Google Surveys, with multiple-choice or open-ended questions, Likert-scale items, or a combination. Often these decisions are based on your resources, time, and goals. Teachers may collect documentation from their classrooms, and other administrative staff can help coordinate, disseminate, and collate the information gathered from the surveys and various environmental rating scales. When all the information is gathered and organized meaningfully, it should be analyzed and reviewed by the director, teachers, and families.

Action Planning and Goal Setting

Every program assessment and improvement plan has a starting point, or baseline. As discussed in Chapter 2, reading your program and identifying its strengths, needs, resources, and obstacles are part of a strategic or action planning process. This is a time to both celebrate your progress and identify areas for improvement. From here, you can develop your short- and long-term goals for the year. A long-term goal may be to increase family engagement. A short-term goal to help you get there may be to provide a variety of times for family meetings and events to allow for more participation. Often there will be several short-term goals to help you reach the long-term goal. Once you have your long-term goals, the program assessment plan will help you determine if you are meeting them.

How Am I Doing? Evaluating the Director

Asking your program constituents—staff and families among them—to evaluate your performance and effectiveness as director can be intimidating but valuable. There are various instruments available that can be completed by staff, consultants, policymakers, and others to formally measure and benchmark a director's practices, such as the *Program Administration Scale* (PAS). Informal, open-ended questionnaires that you create and tailor to your specific needs can also provide valuable information. Are you most interested in receiving feedback about the program's culture? Or how effective your communication strategies are? Perhaps you'd like staff to share their thoughts on how training and professional development are handled. Think about the kind of information you hope to gain from an evaluation and which type of tool will coax the highest response rate from staff and families. Regardless of the assessment you use, it is important to do the following:

> Provide the option to submit feedback anonymously. You may receive more candid ideas.

> Be open to the feedback. While some comments may make you feel defensive, make a concentrated effort to consider what is being said instead of how it is being said.

> Feel comfortable sharing and discussing the results with your supervisor (if you have one), colleagues, or your mentor. Talking things through with someone outside the program can often provide another perspective.

> Come up with some next steps for improvement. Express your appreciation for the feedback to the community and share some possible new goals.

> Repeat this process at least annually. As new families and staff join, learning goals shift, and other aspects of the center evolve, it is important to keep your finger on the pulse of the program community.

Directly from a Director

I was nervous to have teachers and families assess my performance as director, but in the end, their feedback was really helpful. Some teachers shared that they would like me to observe their classrooms more frequently. The music teacher wanted to connect more with classroom curriculum. Families wanted more opportunities to meet with me. Knowing what people needed most from me helped focus where to place and improve my efforts to support them.

Assessing What Children Are Learning

Assessment of children's work and growth is another area that directors and teachers must consider. While it is the teachers' responsibility to focus on individual children, you need to keep the big picture in mind and develop an assessment plan that connects with your program's values, goals, and curriculum approach. The assessment plan should answer the questions "How do children show what they know?" and "How can we best determine what children are learning and what they are ready to learn next?"

Some programs choose standard assessment tools, such as COR Advantage and The Work Sampling System, to use with children at certain checkpoints throughout the year. Such assessment tools are commonly linked to specific curriculum models; for example, COR Advantage is linked to the HighScope Curriculum, and the assessment program Teaching Strategies GOLD is linked to The Creative Curriculum. These assessments can be time consuming, but they are useful in maintaining consistency across the center. They also provide a helpful framework for teachers who are less experienced with child development and assessment, easing the director's burden in developing a system that works for everyone.

Other programs create an assessment portfolio for each child. These portfolios can include

> Children's work samples from throughout the year

> Teachers' observation notes

> Photos of children's work

> Children's reflections on their work

In some cases, the portfolio moves with the child to the next year of her education. In order for the portfolio to serve as a comprehensive record of a child's learning and development, teachers should also take the time to label children's work and document the child's thoughts and comments about her own work. In other words, a portfolio is not just a collection of work but a very intentionally curated compilation that clearly demonstrates certain aspects of a child's developmental growth and progress. Portfolios also offer an opportunity to help children reflect on their own learning. A teacher might ask a child to review some of her work samples and think about which ones she's most proud of and why, or what she learned while doing the activity or work. Teachers also ask children to select some of the items to include in their portfolio.

Families are partners in their children's assessment process. Provide opportunities for them to share input into the goals they have for their children through intake forms and conferences and other formal meetings. Keep in mind that teachers and families may not always attach the same importance to particular goals for children. A teacher may feel that a family's goal—which they have expressed is very important to them—is not developmentally appropriate. However, differences of opinion present opportunities for discussion, mutual listening, and learning about each other's perspectives. Develop strategies for documenting and communicating this information in a professional and thoughtful way with families, and make yourself available for discussion with teachers or families if differences do arise.

Assessment Methods

Methods for assessing what children know and can do fall on a continuum from formal to informal (Epstein et al. 2004). On one end are standardized tests that are *norm referenced*—meaning "a child's performance is interpreted by comparing it to the performance of a group of peers, or *norming group*, who have previously taken the same test" (Bodrova & Leong 2018, 18). Such tests are often used to obtain and report information about children's development for the purpose of program evaluation and funding. Norm-referenced screening instruments may be used to identify potential sensory, cognitive, or social and emotional challenges as part of a child's ongoing assessment in a program. A formal evaluation is often initiated when a child's teacher or family has questions about the child's development and wants to identify potential delays or disabilities and make a referral for specialized services.

Authentic assessment appears on the more informal end of the assessment continuum. It is the ongoing process of gathering evidence about children's learning, development, performance, and understanding that is used to guide planning and instruction (Bagnato, Neisworth, & Pretti-Frontczak 2010). It involves observing and documenting children's learning in the context of their daily activities and routines. The figure on pages 88–89 identifies the various components of authentic assessment. This information is important for both directors and teachers to understand. While teachers are directly implementing these practices with children, you need to make intentional decisions to support them in using these approaches appropriately and effectively.

It is best practice to make sure families have reviewed the program's assessment plan and have an opportunity to raise concerns about any part of it. Remember that "high-stakes decisions about a child" should never be based on just one formal evaluation (Riley-Ayers 2018, 2). A comprehensive, holistic view of the child—including, when appropriate, culturally and linguistically appropriate standardized assessment tools—should be used.

Components of Authentic Assessment

	Some Questions to Focus on	**Tools**
Monitor Keep track of the child's learning experiences	› What projects has he participated in? › What materials did he use? › How does he approach learning?	› Checklists › Inventories › Class lists › Journal entries
Observe Gather information about the child by watching and listening	› Note general impressions of the child. › How does she interact with others? › Is she engaged with the activity?	› Systematic observations › Anecdotal records › Running records (noting all behaviors a child exhibits to help determine their thinking process) › Audio and video recordings › Photographs
Interact Find out what the child knows, feels, believes, and understands	› Ask clarifying and probing questions to better understand the child's thinking. › Challenge the child's current thinking and help him move beyond where he is.	› Questioning techniques (Why do you think . . . ? What if . . . ? Tell me more about . . . . I wonder . . .) › Interviews › Checklists › Response journals
Analyze Gather and review artifacts of the child's learning; seek family's input	› What evidence do you have to demonstrate the child's learning and progress? › When examining artifacts, consider both content and process. › What does the child's family see her doing at home and in the community?	› Written or dictated stories and reports › Writing and drawing samples › Audio and video recordings › Portfolios › Photographs › Rubrics › Family surveys › Conversations with family at home or in the center

	Some Questions to Focus on	Tools
Report Organize the data in a meaningful way and share it with the family, director, and others	› Involve the child in this process by asking questions (Which drawing of your block construction would you like me to put in your portfolio? Why this one? Tell me more about this drawing).	› Family conferences › Progress reports › Narratives about the child written by the teacher › Self-assessment › Portfolios › Rubrics
Link to instruction Use the data to inform instruction and practice	› Ask questions to improve individualized teaching strategies (How can I use the child's interest in robots to engage her during circle time? Would this child be more likely to spend longer periods of time in the language arts center if I included more books about foxes?).	› All of the above

What Is Documentation?

Documentation is the process of systematically "observing, recording, interpreting, and sharing" evidence of children's learning (Krechevsky et al. 2013, 59). Teachers document children's work in a number of ways, including collecting drawing and writing samples, taking photographs of a structure made outdoors with natural materials, noting observations of a child's processes or interactions, making audio or video recordings of dramatic play scenarios, or transcribing a child's thoughts and questions about her own work. To be useful, documentation must be intentional and planned. Effective documentation makes children's learning visible in ways that help inform educators', parents', and policymakers' understanding of and reflection on children's development and thinking processes. While documenting children's learning is primarily a responsibility of teachers, your leadership and support of them in this process are critical to its usefulness.

Beyond recording and evaluating children's work, documentation has many benefits. It serves as a way to revisit experiences and extend thinking for children. It helps teachers plan curriculum because it links observation, planning, implementation, and assessment. For program leaders, it's also a way to communicate and share what is going on in the center and the classroom with others (children, families, teachers, and the community). Documentation can bring people together in a diverse community, celebrate similarities and differences, and create a shared history.

Families especially appreciate seeing tangible evidence of their children's learning process, as in the following vignette:

Marisol is a 5-year-old in Penelope's preschool class at Sandy Shore Playgroup. At pickup time one afternoon, Marisol's grandfather, Oscar, remarks to the program director, Isla, that he doesn't think Marisol is "really learning anything" and that he is worried that she won't be ready for kindergarten. Isla suggests that the two of them and Penelope meet to discuss his concerns. Before the meeting, Isla and Penelope discuss how to best explain the program's curriculum to Marisol's grandfather. As part of this preparation, they also review the portfolio and documentation Penelope has compiled about Marisol over the last few months and select pieces to share with her family.

At the meeting, they give Oscar an overview of the program's curriculum approach and how it connects to the program's learning goals and state standards. What really seems to convince him of Marisol's progress and puts him at ease are the samples of documentation they show him. There is a short story partly written and partly dictated by Marisol about her thoughts on one of her favorite books, *Strega Nona*, by Tomie dePaola, as well as photos showing her

creating her own art based on the book's illustrations. Finally, there is an anecdotal narrative written by Penelope about her observation that Marisol understood the story plot and was able to express her thoughts orally and in writing (language and literacy skills). Penelope also noted Marisol's attention to detail as she carefully mimicked the original artwork in her own drawing (creative expression and fine motor skills). Oscar beams with pride for his granddaughter as he pores over these materials, even seeming a little surprised at the complexity of thought Marisol's work shows. At the end of the meeting, he tells Isla and Penelope that he looks forward to seeing more documentation during the year.

Directly from a Director

Learning how to document is a skill that needs to be practiced. The more you do it, the more focused and fine-tuned your observation skills will become.

Moving Toward a Culture of Documentation

If the teachers in your program do not already document children's work, they might be resistant or feel it is just one more thing they need to work into an already full routine. It's your responsibility to discuss the merits of the practice and listen to teachers' input in order to collectively adopt and establish a culture of documentation. The following will help you support and collaborate with the teachers in this process:

> **Create an atmosphere where teachers feel comfortable exploring and experimenting with different methods of documentation to figure out what works best for them.** For example, with your encouragement, a teacher might try recording a video and taking photos before she discovers that writing a learning story—a short, narrative story about what she observed—about the small group of children taking apart an old, broken toy to see how it works is the approach that best helps her reflect on the children's interests and how she can extend their learning.

> **Provide the necessary tools, time, and support.** To make documentation an integral part of the program, teachers need convenient access to tools (e.g., computers, digital cameras, printers, display boards). Documentation takes time, practice, and focus. If you ask teachers to create individual portfolios and high-quality documentation, they need dedicated time to do this work.

> **Offer direction and structure to the process, as needed.** Some teachers may feel overwhelmed with the documentation process or unsure of where to start. Provide samples or templates for documentation displays, portfolios, and newsletters.

Whether you're introducing documentation to your program or simply trying to improve its effectiveness, ask teachers to consider what they are documenting and why. The subject and goal should be identified first, and then the documentation format can be considered—perhaps it works better as an entry in the child's journal rather than a wall display. Determine if the documentation will simply be descriptive or also include an analysis of what's being observed. Encourage teachers to consider how the documentation can be interactive and invite feedback. Will children review the documentation and share their thoughts on what happened? How might families share their feedback?

Practical Tips for Facilitating Documentation

> Establish documentation policies and procedures that cover confidentiality and uploading, handling, and sharing photographs and other files securely.

> If you expect teachers to use technology, such as recording devices and editing software, provide them with appropriate training.

> Facilitate use of the center's common areas and other shared spaces outside of individual classrooms (e.g., hallways, reception areas, the staff lunch room) for teachers to take turns using as strategic locations to display documentation.

> Technology can sometimes make it too easy to indiscriminately take a lot of photos or record reams of dialogue and lose sight of what is important. Emphasize quality over quantity. Remind teachers to pause before snapping a photograph and ask themselves some questions: What is a good photo? What kind of documentation is meaningful? Who is the documentation for? How can we use our materials with care?

> Documentation does not need to be a time-consuming venture. Just taking time to reflect on practice and experiences in the classroom is valuable. For example, at one center, classroom teachers took turns at each staff meeting bringing a piece of student work, such as a child's drawing, to have a group discussion about it. If teachers need some prompting, ask questions like "What do you notice in the drawing?," "What do you think the child was thinking about?," and "What are your next steps?"

One director explained the process she used to include documentation in her program: "After we made the schoolwide decision to make documentation a collective focus, we had many workshops and discussions about documentation at our monthly staff meetings, head teacher meetings, and retreats. It became a professional development priority. I realized it was important to create an environment that allowed people to take risks, try new ideas, make mistakes, and try again. Teachers were given permission to mess around and do different things. We gave every class a digital camera. It was only then that we realized there are no-, low-, and high-tech documentation methods and there are benefits to each. There is documentation that is beautifully mounted and planned, and there is quick and dirty documentation, the end-of-the-day message written on newsprint or on a white board. All kinds of documentation have value."

You can use documentation to invite input from all constituencies. Provide sticky notes and a pencil next to a documentation panel so viewers can note their reactions and questions about the documentation. For example, you might give children the opportunity to create self-portraits and answer prompts asking them to describe themselves, such as their interests ("I like _____ ") or something more open ended they choose to share ("One thing you should know about me is _____ "). Together, the self-portraits and self-descriptions can be assembled into a documentation display that celebrates differences and individuality, inspires self-esteem, and encourages conversation and excitement—both in the center hallways and in the wider program community.

While documentation requires you to invest time and resources, the benefits show the practice's worth. It serves as an equal exchange among all members of the school community and is the representation of a loving community that cares for children, families, and teachers alike.

Both program and child assessment are vital processes for measuring your program's effectiveness, ensuring its continued advancement toward the mission and goals you've set, and supporting children's learning and development. Work closely with constituents to understand the different types of assessment to help you identify the right ones for your program.

Big-Picture Takeaways

> Through observation and assessment, you collect data on what is working and not working in your program and then develop goals for program improvement. Collecting and analyzing program data should involve all the program constituencies.

> As director, you are responsible for overseeing the child assessment system used for monitoring children's learning. Usually this is a combination of culturally and linguistically appropriate authentic assessment and standardized assessments.

> Documentation can be used to facilitate the curriculum and to communicate the children's learning and development with families and others in a visually based, engaging way.

Go Deeper

Pedagogical Documentation in Early Childhood: Sharing Children's Learning and Teachers' Thinking, by S. Stacey (Redleaf Press, 2015)

The Power of Observation: Birth to Age 8, Second Edition, by J.R. Jablon, A.L. Dombro, and M.L. Dichtelmiller (Teaching Strategies, 2007)

Spotlight on Young Children: Observation and Assessment, edited by H. Bohart and R. Procopio (NAEYC, 2018)

Chapter Seven

>> Staffing

What the teachers achieved was always more important than what I achieved.

—John Nimmo, personal communication

Your staff is the backbone of your early childhood program. You have many staffing responsibilities: creating a staffing model, scheduling, hiring, retaining, supervising, mentoring, and training, to name only a few! For each of these, you must carefully consider what works best for your specific program.

Staffing Models and Scheduling

A *staffing model* is used to coordinate the quantity and quality of staff members and other resources you need for your day-to-day operations, helping you hire, supervise, and train staff to keep your program running smoothly and efficiently. Many different factors inform your staffing model and decisions, including maintaining licensing ratios, the number of children present in the center at different times of day, coverage for breaks and lunches, overlaps between shifts, and time for preparation and cleanup after the children leave at the end of the day. Ideally, every group of children should have at least two adults present in the classroom. If numbers are low at the beginning or end of the day, there should be at least one other qualified person in the center in case of emergencies. You also need to determine the qualifications your teachers should have. For example, does each class in your program require two coteachers with similar qualifications and responsibilities or one experienced lead teacher and one assistant teacher with less experience and a lighter load of responsibilities?

Clearly define the role of each staff member in your program and create or update a detailed job description for each that you include in the staff handbook. These job descriptions should include the title as well as a comprehensive list of that role's expected responsibilities. Staff roles are identified by different terminology across the country. Some programs use the term *teacher* to refer to anyone who is in the classroom day to day with children, while others differentiate by qualifications and responsibilities. Here are some common roles in early childhood programs:

> **Lead teacher:** a primary classroom teacher and a mentor to assistant teachers; also called *head teacher* or *mentor teacher*

> **Coteacher:** a fully qualified teacher who leads a classroom jointly with another teacher; together, they share equal responsibility for the group of children in their classroom

> **Assistant teacher:** assists the lead teacher with curriculum, classroom management, and communicating with families; also called *associate teacher*

> **Multiclassroom teacher:** a teacher who is hired to help among the center's various classrooms as needed rather than a single, specific classroom; can serve as a substitute, cover during breaks, or provide additional support for a specific activity or child

> **Aide:** may be hired on a provisional or part-time basis for specific instructional tasks, such as supporting a child with a disability; this title is sometimes also used for an individual who assists in the classroom under close supervision

> **Administrative staff:** provide various program functions and support in capacities outside of classroom instruction; roles might include assistant director, bookkeeper, cook, custodian, enrollment coordinator, nurse, and secretary

> **Consultant:** a professional brought into the program to provide skills and expertise that may not be part of the skillset of your current staff; this individual can be brought in for a specific issue or hired on an ongoing basis. Consultants may include behavior specialists, speech-language pathologists, occupational therapists, physical therapists, and social workers.

When a staff member transitions into a different role in the program, it's best practice to review the description of the new role before they begin. An organizational chart, as described in Chapter 3, is helpful to clearly outline who reports to whom. In some centers, the program leader directly supervises all staff. In others, a director might delegate some direct supervisory responsibilities, such as having lead teachers primarily supervise assistant teachers. Having all of this information readily available will ease another important staffing function that falls to you—hiring.

Hiring Great Teachers

One of the secrets of being an effective director and program leader is surrounding yourself with highly qualified, motivated colleagues. So how do you go about finding them?

Consider the Qualifications and Qualities You Need and Want

The first step in the hiring process is knowing what you're looking for. Review the description of each staff role and consider the following (Schmidt 2017):

> What educational qualifications are required?

> What is the minimum acceptable amount of practical experience?

> What skills are needed to handle the outlined responsibilities?

In addition to these professional requirements, it's critical to consider a candidate's personality and attitude. You can always coach teachers to help them improve their classroom knowledge and skills (addressing challenging behaviors, developing curriculum plans, leading group times), but you can't

Directly from a Director

When I hire, I look not only for understanding and knowledge, but also for how *passionate* someone is about their work. I value the teacher's disposition. I want teachers who are reflective thinkers, ask good questions, have a sense of humor, and are able to let the small stuff go. Most of all, I want lifelong learners—the best teachers are also learners.

always teach them to have a positive attitude, which makes for more collegial relationships, stronger role models for children, and a more enjoyable workplace experience. As the adage goes, "Hire for character, train for skill." It is also important to take into account if the candidate is a good fit for the program and with other staff members with whom they will work every day. Does she believe in the program's philosophy? Do his attitude and style of teaching mesh well with those of the coteacher he will be closely working with?

Advertising for Applicants

Based on the considerations above, create an advertisement for an open position with your contact details and information on how to apply. You can publicize the advertisement in a number of ways, including in print (e.g., local newspapers, community newsletters) or online (e.g., your program's website, job search engines and boards). Local universities often have career websites where you can post the position, or you might send the listing directly to faculty members in the education or child development department. You can also scout for applicants at job fairs and open houses. Often, the most effective and inexpensive way to advertise is through networking. Reach out to current program staff, your contacts in the community, and professional organizations, such as your local Association for the Education of Young Children Affiliate, and ask if they might help you publicize the vacancy through online listservs, websites, social media, and any other outlets they might have at their disposal. Some programs also offer incentives to current staff members for referring candidates that are hired, such as a bonus, additional vacation time, or other benefits.

Interviewing Candidates

After narrowing down the pool of applicants, your next step is to interview the candidates. The process will look something like this:

> **Pre-interview.** A quick 5- to 15-minute conversation by phone is a good way to get a feel for the candidate and for the candidate to get a better sense of the program's needs. This way, you'll be able to gauge whether a more formal, in-person interview makes sense for both you and the candidate.

> **Face-to-face interview with the director.** Schedule time for the candidate to meet with you individually as well as with others in the program. An individual interview provides one-on-one interaction and an opportunity to get to know the candidate in a more informal way that might not reveal itself in a group interview. This part of the process might occur at the beginning of the interview process or at the end. The figure on page 100 shows several sample questions you might ask a candidate in this setting or during a group interview.

> **Face-to-face group interview.** Have the candidate meet with other constituents in the program, including teachers and family representatives, so they can ask the candidate questions. This interview may last 30–45 minutes.

> **Working interview.** Many programs also want to observe the candidate in a classroom to get an idea of her teaching style. In this situation, be clear with the candidate about her role. You want to see the candidate interact with children, such as leading a small group activity or lesson, and perhaps with another teacher, not just observe. That said, candidates should not be asked to change diapers, take children to the bathroom, or anything else that should be conducted only by program staff. Afterward, discuss the experience with the candidate, asking how she felt the lesson went and whether there is anything she would do differently. Take time to also talk with the classroom teacher so he can share his thoughts and feedback about the candidate with you.

Hiring is one of the most important decisions a director can make, and investing the time you need to interview candidates is key. Block off dedicated time for yourself as well as any other staff members involved in the interviewing process.

Sample Interview Questions

General and Personal

› Tell me a little about yourself.

› What drew you to the early childhood education field?

› What about our program interests you most?

› What makes you the best candidate for this position?

› What part of being an early childhood teacher gives you the most satisfaction?

› What part of doing this work is the most challenging for you?

Curriculum

› If I were to walk into your classroom and observe an early math or literacy activity, what would I see?

› Give an example of how you develop a curriculum plan.

› How do you meet the needs of a wide range of learners in your classroom?

› What is an appropriate curriculum plan for infants and toddlers?

› Tell us about one of your favorite group time activities to do with the children and why you enjoy it.

Classroom and Behavior Management

› Tell us about your classroom management style and strategies you use to guide children's behavior.

› Give an example of an experience you've had working with a child with a challenging behavior and how you addressed it.

Working with Families and Colleagues

› Tell us about experiences you have had working with families.

› What kinds of conflicts have you dealt with? How did you handle the conflict?

› How do you engage families in the classroom?

› How do you convey difficult information to families?

› Have you ever had a conflict with a colleague or supervisor? If so, how did you resolve it?

Retaining Great Teachers

Once you find and hire teachers, how do you keep them? High turnover is a big challenge in this field, one that costs a program both time and money. Key factors that contribute to job turnover include job satisfaction, salary, benefits, job commitment, stress, burnout, and work environment (Schwarz et al. 2003). As the early childhood field raises qualification and certification requirements, the median hourly wage for teachers in early care and education settings is 39.3 percent below the median hourly wage of workers in other occupations (Gould 2015). Doing what you can to offer your staff a livable wage is a key factor in retaining qualified teachers. Whenever possible, allocate funds in your budget for other staff incentives like professional development, travel to conferences, and purchasing equipment and materials.

There are also structural supports that may increase retention. Some ideas include

> Taking the time to fully orient new teachers. Providing adequate preparation and training is an important part of making teachers feel both capable in their role and welcome to the program community.

> Giving teachers control over a small classroom budget for materials and supplies

> Respecting teachers' planning time and other scheduled events

> Supporting your teachers when they are dealing with an issue like a child with a challenging behavior or a difficult family communication situation. This support can be emotional reinforcement as well as practical suggestions.

> Offering exciting professional development opportunities

Strive to create a positive, collaborative atmosphere where teachers are viewed as stakeholders, not just employees. Valuing staff members' opinions and making them feel appreciated go a long way toward fostering a positive environment. It's also important to learn how each staff member prefers to be recognized. Not everyone, for example, wants a big shout-out at a staff meeting; some would prefer positive feedback that is shared more privately. One director has a goal of walking through her center once a week to look for examples of good things happening in each classroom—an innovative curriculum technique, an inspiring learning moment, a collaborative effort between a teacher and a family member. She acknowledges staff personally via email and more publicly at monthly staff meetings. The key point is to find small, specific moments to celebrate regularly.

Play is an essential part of children's learning and development, but it also has major benefits for adults, including reducing stress and absenteeism while increasing productivity, creativity, camaraderie, and morale, all of which make for happier employees (BrightHR & Robertson Cooper Ltd. 2015). And a happy staff means a lower turnover rate. Here are just a few ideas to create a fun, playful work environment:

> Start or end staff meetings with an activity like human knot, pop culture trivia, or telephone.

> Acknowledge all staff birthdays each month with a cake in the kitchen and a card naming everyone who has a birthday that month.

> Once a month, hold a $1.00 staff raffle with prizes like a gift certificate to a local restaurant, a pair of movie tickets, and a manicure and pedicure. (Ask local businesses to donate or discount the prizes.)

> Leave small token gifts (e.g., pins, notes with inspirational quotes, a favorite candy, candles) in staff mailboxes as a surprise every so often.

> Have a peer recognition board where teachers can write congratulatory, appreciative, or generally positive comments about their colleagues' accomplishments for others to see. (When appropriate, you might allow families the opportunity to contribute to the board as well.)

Communicating with Staff

As touched on in Chapter 2, open, honest, and clear communication is the foundation of your relationship with program staff. It is not just a matter of keeping staff informed or sending a well-written email. Communication should be respectful *and* reciprocal, meaning everyone engages in talking and listening. As director, you should serve as a valuable resource for your staff, but that will be the case only if they feel comfortable enough to approach you. Their level of comfort is guided by their experiences in interacting with you, from the words you use (verbal communication) to your tone and body language (nonverbal communication) to your respect for the confidential nature of matters they discuss with you.

Regular interaction—face-to-face or written, one-on-one or in a group setting—is critical to a program's effective operation. There are many ways to communicate with your staff: write a personal handwritten note to acknowledge progress made in difficult situations, meet with a teaching team to help them problem solve a classroom issue, or publicly share a parent's compliment during a staff meeting. As one director explained, "It's really important how feedback to teachers is phrased and how it's communicated. When I see an area in need of improvement, I don't just tell my teachers what to do, and I certainly don't send it via email. Instead, I might schedule a time to briefly meet in person and say, 'How are things going? Is there any part of your day that is tricky that I can help with?' I want my teachers to engage, and eventually initiate, these conversations so that they understand my goal is to be supportive rather than critical."

Team-Building Activities

There are a number of activities and exercises that can help you understand your staff's group dynamics. Here are a few activities to use with your whole staff at the beginning of the year or whenever there are a number of new staff:

Compass Points

In this activity, each compass direction represents a preferred personal working style when in a group. For example, *north* represents someone who likes to take initiative or immediate action; *east*, someone who thoughtfully plans before acting; *south*, someone who is an inclusive collaborator; and *west*, someone who is a creative risk taker (Turner & Greco 2001). Invite your staff to indicate which compass point best represents their own style by moving to a certain spot in the room. Through this exercise, staff members are encouraged to reflect on how they work best, information that is also helpful for colleagues—and a director—to know.

Two Truths and a Lie

Each participant writes down three things about herself—two that are true and one that is fabricated. Take 10 to 15 minutes for the group to talk in an open format, sharing information that leads others to believe that the untrue fact they've written is actually true. Afterwards, gather in a circle and have each person take a turn to share each of the statements she's written about herself. The group then votes on which statement they think is the lie, and the person reveals what was true and what was false. This game is a fun way to help work colleagues get to know each other better.

Use What You've Got

In advance, create a project or challenge for staff that includes a goal they must work together to accomplish within clear boundaries (e.g., limited supplies, a set time limit). For example, you might ask each team to create a structure that can hold up a person or to move an object across the room without directly touching it. Divide your staff members at random into small groups of equal sizes and ask them to meet the objective, working cooperatively and utilizing each other's strengths.

Teacher Observation and Evaluation

Directly from a Director

How can teachers know their strengths and how to improve if their director doesn't help them learn how to be more effective? It might be hard to discuss, but it's important to be honest and constructive in your evaluation and feedback.

Observing teachers to evaluate the quality and effectiveness of their work and providing feedback is an important part of improving their practice and, ultimately, improving the program. Your program should have a uniform process for teacher observations. Before conducting an observation, sit down with the teacher to identify the goals of the observation and ask if there is anything the teacher wants specific feedback on. During the observation, take detailed notes about what you see and conversations you hear, verbatim when possible. (For example, how does Cora respond when one of the toddlers in her classroom starts crying as her dad leaves at drop-off time? What does Cora do? What does she say to the child?)

After the observation, once you have had time to review and analyze your notes, talk with the teacher about the observation. You should visit classrooms and provide informal feedback to teachers at least twice a month. Ideally, conduct formal teacher observations at least twice a year. When writing a staff member's annual evaluation, reflect on these observations and the growth they demonstrate the staff member achieving over the last year.

Sample Teacher Observation Form

Teacher: Darwishi (Lead Teacher)   **Date:** January 23   **Time:** 9:00 a.m.

Classroom: Preschool

Lesson: Group time book talk, *Pete the Cat: I Love My White Shoes*

Observed by: Fiorella (Director)

Observation Notes	Comments About What Worked	Suggestions/Questions
• Teacher (T.) begins singing circle song to gather children to mats; children (C.) sit down quickly • T. introduces book, *Pete the Cat: I Love My White Shoes* • (Verbatim conversation between T. and C.) T.: "What do you notice about Pete the cat?" C.: "He is blue," and "He has shoes on his feet." T.: "I wonder why Pete has shoes on his feet." • T. reads book; at end of story, C. jump up and down and run to grab books off shelves • T. "Everyone sit down. Now, let's play a game with our shoes." • T. sings song, "Old Shoes, New Shoes," and everyone responds with their shoe color	• C. knew routine to go to circle mats when song is sung • T. asked open-ended questions to get C. interested in book • T. used a lot of expression and gestures when reading book • C. very engaged during book reading • Great choice of book for this age group • Liked the way T. connected the book to another shoe song and let the children personalize it	**Suggestions** C. were very excited after book was over and had a lot of energy. For a smoother transition at end of story, try asking C. to dance to the "I Love My White Shoes" song. Either have the CD loaded and ready to go or the audio file queued up on your phone or computer so you can just press play. After the dance party, ask the C. to sit down and transition to the "Old Shoes, New Shoes" song and activity. **Questions** • Why did you choose this book? • What were your goals and objectives for this activity?

Teacher Comments: I chose this book because I like the chanting refrain, and the children in my class are very interested in singing and books with repetition. My goals were for children to learn more about colors and to connect the shoe theme in the book and the song.

Here is a condensed outline of the teacher observation process:

Before the Observation

> Identify the goals of the observation.

> Ask the teacher what areas of professional development in particular she is seeking guidance on and what questions she has about her teaching.

During the Observation

> Conduct your observation during different times (morning or afternoon) and for varying intervals of time (30 minutes to an hour).

> Be attentive and minimize distractions.

> Record what you see: What works? What is challenging for the teacher? What suggestions do you have? (See the figure on page 105 for sample observation notes.)

After the Observation

> Meet with the teacher to provide face-to-face feedback.

- Ask the teacher for his thoughts on how the lesson went before you share your feedback: What did he feel went well? What would he do differently?

- Talk about what you noticed, beginning with positive things you observed.

- Introduce your concerns by asking about situations you saw as challenging for the teacher. Use data and specific examples you noted to illustrate your points ("What did you think about the difficulty Mitchell and Damon had sharing the blocks this morning?"). This provides you with an entry point to share your thoughts and comments.

- Provide your suggestions and recommendations for immediate action (e.g., rearranging the equipment so children can better access materials) and long-term action (e.g., suggested readings, observing other classrooms, attending professional development trainings).

> Write up a clean, final copy of your observation notes and your notes from the meeting while these interactions are fresh in your mind. Give a copy to the teacher for his personal records and include a copy in his file.

Supervising Teachers

In addition to evaluation, good supervision includes mentoring, coaching, and encouraging reflective practice. There are two kinds of supervision. *Operational supervision* refers to the day-to-day logistical tasks that keep an organization running, such as planning and monitoring the teachers' workload,

evaluating the quality of work, administration, and record keeping. *Developmental supervision*, on the other hand, focuses on the education and professional development of staff. Mentoring, coaching, and reflective practice, defined below, fall into the second category of supervision. The figure on page 108 compares both supervision techniques.

Mentoring takes many forms and can be a formal or informal process. An educator might be matched with a more experienced professional in the field to serve as a mentor who gives feedback about teaching practices, offers advice about professional development strategies, helps set career goals, assists in establishing contacts to build a solid network, and exchanges ideas to use in the classroom. A mentor might be from a different organization than his mentee. Mentoring is a valuable way to help teachers grow personally and professionally. Your role is to help each teacher in your program identify a mentor, either within the program or outside of it. You might serve as a mentor yourself.

Operational Supervision Versus Developmental Supervision Techniques

	Type of Support	Example
Operational Supervision	Helping staff meet the expectations of their job descriptions as described in staff handbook	Review the program's policies on safety procedures at the staff meeting as a refresher prior to a fire drill.
Developmental Supervision	Supporting the growth and development of staff in skill, knowledge, and disposition	Sit in on family–teacher conferences to observe how the teacher shares potentially unwelcome information about a child's behavior after the teacher self-identifies this as an area of improvement. Afterward, provide your thoughts and feedback.
› Mentoring	Providing career development advice and emotional support	Connect a newly hired assistant infant and toddler teacher with a well-established lead infant and toddler teacher.
› Coaching	Teaching specific skills and strategies in a nonevaluative process	Brainstorm possible questions and language to use at a family–teacher conference when a challenging behavior needs to be discussed.
› Reflective Practice	Guiding staff in reflecting on their actions and experiences to improve their professional practices	Review the child portfolios a preschool teacher has maintained for the last couple months. Prompt him to reflect on why he chose to include certain works, if he involved the children in the selection process, whether he shared any of its contents with children's families and if and how in thinking about his process during each of these steps, he would do anything differently.

Coaching is a method of improving individual or team performance through direction and instruction to learn a particular skill or work toward a specific goal. Coaches often observe teachers in the classroom and provide feedback before and after instruction in a particular skillset. For example, a teacher may ask for more support around the transition time between group time and outdoor play. As a coach, the director can help the teacher clarify what exactly needs to happen between group time and outdoor play (e.g., children put away their mats, get their jackets, line up by the door). Together, the teacher and director analyze what is not working (e.g., too many children in cubby area at the same time) and develop some new strategies for dismissing children from circle time (e.g., sending children three or four at a time to put away their mats, put on their jackets, and line up). The coach does not provide answers; instead, she helps the teacher come up with ideas to implement and offers feedback.

Reflective practice is a strategy that involves systematically thinking about your actions and experiences to improve your professional practices. Schön (1983) identifies two key ways to do this:

> Reflection *in* action, which involves thinking on your actions, experiences, and motivations in the moment to consider what you can do next (immediate implementation).

> Reflection *on* action, which involves thinking on your actions, experiences, and motivations after they occur to consider what you could change or do differently next time (future implementation).

You can lead teachers in engaging in this practice by prompting them with self-reflective questions. For example, when you share feedback with a teacher after conducting an observation, you may ask, "How do you think the nature exploration activity went?" and "What do you think the children gained from that experience?" If a teacher feels that their instruction went well but you disagree, you can share what you noticed and a question or comment that prompts the teacher to consider what she might have done differently: "You're right, the children were very excited about the activity. It's important that they're engaged, and it's also important that we look for ways to stretch their thinking. You did a great job of acknowledging what they were saying about their discoveries, but I thought there were opportunities you could have taken to build on what they were saying. How do you think you could have taken their learning about the starfish to the next level?" The process of observation and reflection is more effective if the teachers are part of the dialogue and are given the opportunity to think about a new or different approach that would improve their teaching practice for themselves. By guiding teachers to reflect on action, you are helping them hone the skills they can also apply to reflect in action.

Staff Meetings

Staff meetings can be important professional development opportunities—or they can be a waste of everyone's time. During a staff meeting, you might

> **Provide information,** such as an upcoming licensing renewal site visit or changes to program policies.

> **Open the floor for opinions and ideas to be shared.** To revitalize the annual scholarship fundraising event, ask your staff for new ideas and approaches.

> **Solve problems** by facilitating group discussions. What can be done to make end-of-day cleanup take less time?

> **Incorporate skill training.** For example, invite an expert on supporting dual language learners in the classroom to speak and answer some staff questions.

> **Provide a space for teachers to get support** about a specific issue they are dealing with in the classroom or a general concern.

Directly from a Director

I want to make sure that our two-hour staff meetings are useful *and* fun. I need to make sure I include professional development objectives as well as time for our team to connect and build relationships. I always open my staff meetings with an interactive activity that we can all participate in to engage their attention. Then, I have prepared content with an objective to improve our curriculum or relationships with families or to review new regulations.

Effective program leaders proactively plan staff meetings. Think about the monthly meetings you will hold over the course of a year and develop a tentative topic list for each based on your goals and the staff's input. Each meeting should also have some flexible time built in for emergent issues that will inevitably occur. Send out the staff meeting agenda at least a week in advance to allow staff to prepare.

A staff meeting should be a time for sharing, brainstorming, and interacting instead of a one-sided presentation. When planning staff meetings, seasoned directors recommend allowing different staff members to take leadership roles they prepare for, perhaps by sharing specialized expertise on a topic or presenting on activities that are happening in their classrooms. By sharing the spotlight, the conversation becomes less of a top-down approach from the director and more an exchange among the school community. You lead the tone of the meeting, so be sure to keep it positive and free of judgment. You might create a rule that what's discussed at a staff meeting doesn't leave that group of educators and isn't discussed outside of the staff meeting for confidentiality. At the end of

Ideas for Your Staff Meetings

Here are a few ways you might make your next staff meeting engaging, productive, and collaborative:

❯ Case study presentations

Have teachers take turns presenting a case study from their classrooms for discussion. Each case study should focus on a specific child and an aspect of their learning and development. After presenting the case, the teacher invites others to offer suggestions on how to better support the child. The presentation might include documentation samples, such as observation notes, sample student work, and video clips, and often some questions to guide the discussion.

❯ Compliment cards

As staff members arrive at the meeting room, ask them to take an index card, write their name on it, and place it in a basket. Once everyone is in attendance, pass around the basket and ask each person to draw one card and write two complimentary things about the person whose name they've drawn. You can repeat this process a few times. At the end, each person should find the card with her own name and read what others have written. You might invite a few volunteers to read their cards aloud and share their reactions.

❯ Mindmapping

Announce a topic or theme, such as *going green*. Give the group a minute or two to think about what that topic means to them. Then, have each person say what came to mind, whether it's a single word or a complete thought, while you write their responses on a large easel pad. Once everyone has had a chance to contribute, study the responses together and discuss what direction you might be able to take or act on (e.g., starting a recycling program, coordinating a centerwide activity on water conservation, buying children's books about preserving the rainforest, organizing a field trip to a national park).

❯ Round-robin curriculum idea sharing

Ask teachers to come prepared to share their favorite curriculum ideas or discoveries, from a new children's book related to supporting anti-bias education to a new, inexpensive STEM activity. You can specify a different focus each month or let teachers pick anything that excites them or they're passionate about. Along with the curriculum idea, teachers should also share its objectives and outcomes for the children.

the staff meeting, ask for feedback on topics the staff would like covered at the next meeting to ensure that each meeting agenda is as useful and staff driven as possible.

Directly from a Director

If we are going to help new professionals develop their knowledge and job skills, we need to have a plan. I have the teachers in my program fill out a form to identify their goals. Not only does this give them something concrete to work toward, it also helps me consider how I can best help them.

Supporting Your Staff's Professional Development

Professional development refers to the many different types of education and training experiences that support professional growth. For early childhood educators, this includes a wide range of activities and resources, such as books and professional journals, workshops, conferences, online coursework, onsite technical training and assistance, and professional learning communities. As director, you not only establish professional development as something your staff needs and will benefit from, you also provide the support to make these opportunities happen. This could mean helping teachers set personal goals for themselves and offering advice, allocating funds in the budget for conference attendance, and arranging for a professional development provider to come on site to work with your staff in a more personalized way.

Goal Setting to Empower Teachers

Everyone in the organization should have the opportunity to grow their skills and develop their talents as a teacher. One helpful tool for supporting this growth is a professional goal sheet, such as the example at the top of page 113. At the beginning of each year, ask each staff member to fill out this sheet and share it with you. Use the information provided to learn what staff members hope to achieve so you can determine how best to support them. For example, if a teacher sets a professional goal of better serving a Spanish- and English-speaking dual language learner in her class, you might recommend a few journal articles with ideas for teaching strategies and a library blog that talks about new children's picture books available in both English and Spanish. Later, if you find or hear about a local workshop on supporting dual language learners in early childhood, you can encourage the teacher to attend using some of the program's professional development funds.

Professional Goal Sheet

Name: _____   Supervisor: _____

Job Title: _____   Date: _____

List three professional goals you have for the year: _____

_____

_____

What will you do to work on these goals? (These should be specific actions.)_____

_____

_____

What do you need from your supervisor to support your goals? _____

_____

_____

Meet with staff members midway through the year to review their goals and progress together as well as determine if any adjustments should be made to their action plans. At the end of the calendar, fiscal, or school year, ask staff to fill out a self-assessment form, such as the one below, and share it with you. The form should ask staff members to consider their

> Accomplishments in working toward their goals along with areas of strength in their overall job performance

> Challenges they faced in meeting their goals and any areas of development in which they would like to see personal growth

> Performance goals they might like to set for the future

This form is a helpful platform for you to hold one-on-one meetings with your staff members to review their reflections and discuss how you can support their growth and goals. The goal-setting process is part of the bigger staff evaluation process. At the end of the year, the director writes an evaluation of each staff member, adding their thoughts to the information gathered through goal setting and the teacher's self-assessment.

End-of-Year Self-Assessment

Name: _____   Supervisor: _____

Job Title: _____   Date: _____

Strengths/Accomplishments: _____

Challenges/Areas of Growth: _____

New Goals for the Future: _____

Signature of Supervisor: _____   Date: _____

Employee Comments: _____

_____

Employee Signature: _____   Date: _____

Ideas for Effective Professional Development

Effective professional development is more than just relaying information. It must relate not only to the needs of the staff but to their wants.

> **Cultivate buy-in.** Helping staff understand *why* it is essential for them to grow as a professional in the field is essential to their willingness to participate and engagement in the process—in other words, you need to put in the effort to cultivate their buy-in. Staff members should be partners in their professional development. Find out what they need and want by gathering ongoing feedback, either in person or through more anonymous methods such as a survey where staff can list or check off specific workshop topics they are interested in or general areas of growth they want to focus on. Set an example by being mindful of your own professional development as director.

> **Encourage peer observation.** Ask teachers to pair up and identify one aspect of their teaching (e.g., group time, transitions) they would like to improve. Each teacher then observes their partner in the classroom, focusing on the identified issues. Observations can be documented through whatever method the teacher feels fits best. After the observations are conducted, the partnered teachers meet again to share what they noticed and their feedback and suggestions.

> **Coordinate center visits.** Arrange for teachers to visit and observe other programs that excel in a specific area of pedagogy or other topic that is of interest to your teachers. Perhaps a teacher is looking for ways to better arrange her classroom to accommodate a child in a wheelchair. You might send her to observe the classroom environment at a program that includes a number of children with physical disabilities who use assistive devices.

> **Establish a book group.** To keep yourself and staff informed about current educational research and teaching methods, invite teachers to join a group that meets on a regular basis to read and discuss respected literature from the field, from *Young Children* and *Child Care Exchange* articles to a chapter in an early childhood education book. Book groups could also focus on reviewing new children's books and how teachers might connect them to curriculum activities.

> **Get in the classroom.** There is nothing more powerful than walking the talk. Stepping into the classroom to coteach with your staff can provide them with support, mentorship, and collegiality. It is also an opportunity to observe teachers in action firsthand. Some program leaders try to spend an hour in a different classroom each week.

Professional Learning Communities

Another model of professional development is to create a professional learning community (PLC). A *PLC* is a team of educators who meet on a regular basis to share curriculum ideas, teaching strategies, samples of documentation, challenges, and other matters from their classrooms and give each other feedback to improve their practice methods. Guided questions and prompts, called *protocols*, provide conversations with structure and lead to more focused, productive discussions (Krechevsky et al. 2013; Venables 2015).

Typically, PLCs are made up of people in similar professional roles, such as a group of infant and toddler teachers. However, they can also be composed of members with more diverse roles and who work with different age ranges. PLCs can operate across a single center or multiple centers, in person or online. For the most part, the director is not a regular member of a teacher PLC, but she might choose to attend some PLC meetings over the course of the year. Observing and participating in PLCs offer you opportunities to learn about the different issues of each teaching team as well as to provide your own feedback and ideas. You can also see how effectively teachers work together and learn more what supports you need to provide for your teachers, individually and collectively.

One director shared, "Building the professional learning communities in our program was critical to developing a centerwide staff identity and commitment and breaking down communication barriers. I introduced the concept of PLCs during a staff meeting after a few teachers came to me to express the feeling that their curriculum ideas were stale or that they were experiencing a sense of disconnectedness from what their colleagues were doing in the classroom. I left it to the teachers to decide if they wanted to create these groups and how. They started out on a voluntary basis with a single PLC with just a few teachers from classrooms that served different age ranges. Once other staff members saw the value in what their colleagues were doing, everyone wanted to join!

The members ultimately decided to split into smaller, age-based PLCs. What made the experience most meaningful for me to see was that it was a fully collaborative venture in which all teaching and administrative staff members participated equally."

Power to the Profession

In 2016, NAEYC launched Power to the Profession (P2P), a national collaboration with the goal of unifying and professionalizing the early childhood education field. Fifteen national early childhood organizations have formed a taskforce to lead this initiative, working together to build on the various guidelines and standards that programs use nationwide to develop and establish a shared framework of core components, like career pathways, knowledge and competencies, qualifications, and compensation (NAEYC 2018).

You and your staff can learn more about P2P, sign up for regular updates, and get involved by visiting NAEYC.org/profession.

Managing Confrontations, Conflicts, and Challenges with Staff Members

As someone in a leadership role, you are expected to address conflict among staff in healthy, productive ways and guide your staff to satisfactory resolutions. However, this does not mean it is your responsibility to fix each problem yourself. Not only is this method impossible—even inappropriate in some situations—it will not be effective in the long run. Instead, think of your role as that of a facilitator, providing your staff with the tools they need to problem solve and resolve challenges on their own with your support.

Take proactive steps to help reduce conflict and make it more manageable when it occurs. For example, have clearly articulated policies and procedures to provide concrete expectations, responsibilities, processes, and boundaries. As discussed in Chapter 3, with guidelines in the staff handbook, everyone has a common set of rules they are committed to following. Some staff conflicts might be fairly easy to resolve by referring to your program's staff handbook. Other conflicts will not lend themselves to such a clear-cut resolution. Differences in perspective, stress from a demanding workload or outside influences, and incompatible teaching styles or priorities are just a few sources of workplace conflicts that can lead to a strained rapport between staff members. The following vignette illustrates a conflict between two teachers and how the director intervenes:

> Maya and Robin coteach a preschool class at Firefly Bright Early Learning Center. Maya has taught preschoolers at this center for five years, and Robin is a new hire with previous experience as an early childhood teacher.

A few months into the school year, the two are not working well together, and it is starting to have an impact on the children. Maya always tries to take the lead in planning curriculum and classroom routines, treating Robin more like an aide than a coteacher. Whenever Robin tries to make a suggestion, such as sending the weekly classroom newsletter to families via email instead of as printed handouts, Maya never fails to give a reason why she doesn't think it's a good idea. Though Robin understands that Maya did not have a consistent coteacher for months before Robin arrived and that it might be hard for Maya to share responsibility of the classroom, the message Robin feels she is getting over and over is "That's not how we do things here."

Both Maya and Robin visit Uzume, the program director, separately to complain. After hearing both sides, Uzume encourages them to talk through and work out their problems together. She even offers to let them use her office as a private discussion space while she and another teacher provide coverage for their classroom. When the situation does not change much over the next few weeks, Uzume realizes that she needs to meet with the teachers to determine how she can support them in working together better.

It is clear during the meeting that both teachers feel very hurt by the other. Maya feels Robin is criticizing her well-established methods and strategies. Robin feels Maya neither values her input nor sees the classroom as "theirs." Careful not to take sides, Uzume talks them through finding common ground, keeping in mind the program's goal of having consistent teachers in the classroom until the end of the school year. Finally, they come to a compromise they both agree on: Maya will take the lead on half of the class's routines and activities, sticking to what she believes are tried-and-true methods; Robin will take the lead on the other half and try out some of her new ideas.

Maya and Robin's working relationship is more productive after implementing this solution, though still strained. Because of this, Uzume asks each teacher if she would object to being paired with a different coteacher the following year. They agree to this plan, and Uzume considers their personalities and teaching styles in greater depth when matching them each with another teacher who will hopefully be a better fit.

Professional relationship issues can also occur when people jump to conclusions, make assumptions, and fail to communicate. Providing space and time for discussion and different perspectives is critical for people to be heard and feel valued. Dedicate a room or space in your center that staff can specifically use to address their conflicts in private. The room might contain posters or handouts with reminders to staff to identify their feelings and viewpoints clearly and communicate them respectfully. When people feel that there is opportunity for input, even if the outcome is different from what they want, the outcome will be better accepted and followed. When you address conflicts between staff members, above all remember to

> **Be a good listener.** Taking the time to be fully engaged in hearing teachers' struggles or problems is challenging. Do not think about what to say next when you should be intently listening to what is being said. This links to effectively communicating with staff as discussed on page 102 of this chapter.

> **Never take sides, and offer support to all staff involved in the conflict equally.** Unless it is a clear instance of inappropriate or negligent behavior, never take sides in a conflict between staff members. Your role as facilitator is to be as objective as possible while guiding staff to come to their own resolution. You do not want your actions to be misconstrued as favoritism and alienate other staff members in the process.

> **Never avoid conflict.** While it might be tempting, avoiding or outright ignoring conflict between your staff is detrimental to the health and success of your program. Unresolved conflict can polarize your staff, detract from the mission of your program, keep teachers from working effectively with the children, and ultimately result in high-quality teachers resigning from their positions. It's important to address issues right away.

Staff Dismissals: Having to Let Someone Go

No matter how diligent you are during the hiring process, it sometimes happens that an individual is not a good fit for your program. Unless a staff member's actions warrant immediate termination, such as breaking the law or causing someone harm, the decision to dismiss a staff member should come only after a closely supervised and carefully documented period of time during which you explicitly discuss your concerns directly with the staff member, both verbally and in writing. The disciplinary and dismissal procedures outlined in your staff handbook will be your guidelines.

Susanna is a new teacher in the toddler room. She is great with the children, but after the first two months, she starts coming in late. At first, she's late just once or twice a week and only by 10 to 15 minutes, but soon it becomes three or four times a week and up to 30 minutes late without any notice or explanation. This leaves 10 toddlers in the classroom with just the assistant teacher, while Heidi, the director, scrambles to find someone to cover or does it herself. When confronted by Heidi about her tardiness, Susanna will say, "Oh, sorry, the bus was behind schedule" or "I slept through my alarm." Heidi realizes that this situation could eventually endanger the children, and after a few weeks and several conversations with Susanna, she decides that she must let Susanna go.

What should a director in a situation like Heidi's do?

1. If any difficult situations, such as inadequate job performance or repeated tardiness, arise with staff, be sure to keep written, dated, and organized documentation of these situations. Written documentation serves as important evidence if a teacher needs to be dismissed. Document each time the infraction occurs, what happens (e.g., how late the teacher is, whether she has a justifiable reason for being late, what impact it has on the classroom), and how it is handled.

2. Talk with the staff member. Be clear about the policy or expectation she is not meeting and why it is important (e.g., "Our licensing regulations require two toddler teachers to be present in the room with the children at all times for safety reasons. The children, their families, and your colleagues rely on you."). Show the staff member your documentation so she can see just how many times infractions have occurred.

3. If the problem becomes a pattern (e.g., chronic lateness), give a verbal warning. Document the date this warning is given and what is said.

4. If the behavior persists, issue a written warning and file a copy, signed by the staff member, in her personnel file. At this time, you might also place the staff member on a probation period where she must demonstrate improvement. Let the staff member know that this behavior cannot continue, and make it clear the responsibility of the outcome is the employee's—she has the power to change the behavior and retain her position.

5. If the problem does not resolve or the behaviors do not change, you may have no choice other than to proceed with dismissal. Be sure to confirm the circumstances and the appropriate process (e.g., state laws) as needed with your supervisor, board of directors, or your licensor. Have all the necessary documentation organized and prepared prior to speaking to the staff member, including any documentation she might require from her staff file (e.g., copies of certifications).

6. When notifying a staff member of her dismissal, be clear, calm, and direct about the circumstances that led to termination. It is best practice to conduct the termination with a human resources manager or another administrator present to serve as a third-party witness to the proceedings in the event that the fired employee takes legal action. Again, follow the appropriate protocol outlined in your staff handbook, including logistical matters such as collection of program property (e.g., keycards) and allowing the staff member to collect her personal belongings before being escorted off center property.

7. After dismissing a staff member, make sure you know and understand what rights the staff member is entitled to according to your program's policies and local, state, and federal laws, such as continuation of health insurance coverage (COBRA), unemployment insurance, a final paycheck, and severance pay (Beesley 2016).

Putting together a staff of passionate, dedicated people and helping them grow is one of the most rewarding experiences you have as a program leader. Guiding teachers to develop as professionals in the field is parallel to a teacher guiding the children to learn and develop. By creating a program culture that allows staff to be nurtured, take risks, and be empowered, you open the door to forming professional relationships that can continue even long after your staff have moved on.

Big-Picture Takeaways

> Identify the most important qualities you want in your staff before you begin hiring. Craft interview questions that will help you find individuals with those qualities.

> Individual goal setting empowers teachers to take ownership of their professional development, so support them in this process.

> Effective directors turn the inevitable conflicts of an organization into opportunities for problem solving and growth.

Go Deeper

"Leadership: Supporting a New Generation of Early Childhood Professionals" (*Young Children* cluster issue, Vol. 70, No. 2, May 2015)

School Reform Initiative (SRI): www.schoolreforminitiative.org

Supporting Teachers As Learners: A Guide for Mentors and Coaches in Early Care and Education, by M. Whitebook and D. Bellm (Redleaf Press, 2013)

Chapter Eight

Working with Families

No school can work well for children
if parents and teachers do not act in
partnership on behalf of the children's
best interests.

—**Dorothy H. Cohen,** *The Learning Child: Guidelines*
for Parents and Teachers

Julia peeks out shyly from behind her mother's legs, hesitant to enter the classroom. Emily, her new preschool teacher, kneels down beside her and says, "Hi, Julia! It's so nice to see you again. I'm so excited to have you in my class this year."

While Julia briefly meets Emily's gaze, she does not move from her place. Her mother, Kida, rubs her daughter's arm. "Don't you want to say hello to Ms. Emily?" When Julia shakes her head, Kida continues, "I see so many things waiting for you to play with."

"Yes!" says Emily. "Do you remember when I came to visit you at your house a few weeks ago? I had so much fun catching ladybugs and caterpillars with you in the backyard. I set up a few books with pictures of insects and magnifying glasses over on that table for you." When Julia looks in the direction Emily points to, she knows she has her attention. "Your mom also told me that you really like strawberry yogurt, so I made sure to have some for snack time today."

After a pause, Julia steps out from behind her mother and smiles. With a hug and a kiss goodbye, she races over to the science area where Emily set up the insect books and magnifying glasses. She's soon joined by two children, and they begin to look through the pages together, pointing out photographs to each other.

According to theorist Urie Bronfenbrenner (1988), a young child's immediate family and school have the greatest impact on her, in everything from academic skills to social norms and values. Family engagement in the program greatly enhances children's learning and development, which is why developing meaningful, trusting home–school partnerships is critical (NAEYC 2016). Honest two-way communication, cooperation, and collaboration between educators and families is an essential component of the culture and context of your program (see Chapter 2).

Talk with your staff about the importance of home–school partnerships and the positive impact they can have on these relationships. Together, reflect on how all of you

> Make families feel welcome

> Offer a variety of ways families can participate in their children's learning and in other aspects of the program

> Involve families in decisions about their children's care and education

> Act as a support network for families' diverse needs

> Create spaces of collaboration where goals for the children can be shared among families, teachers, and the director

Families and educators have a shared interest in doing what is best for children, and it is by working together that they can best help children succeed in school and beyond.

The Family's Role in Children's Learning and Development

The concept of a family has continued to change over the years for a number of reasons, including evolving family structures and roles; increasing mobility and urbanization; decreasing involvement of extended family; and stress in modern living, to name a few (Angier 2013). Regardless of what form it takes, the family's role as the child's first teacher cannot be underestimated. For the vast majority of children, the home provides their first experiences with a loving adult and is where most of their basic needs (food, clothing, shelter) are met. It is through these nurturing interactions in the home that young children begin to develop a sense of security and, from that security, the confidence to explore the world. Through their family, children also connect with their larger community. Daily routines and experiences with their families, like shopping at the grocery store, visiting the library, and using public transportation, introduce children to the wider world and more social interactions.

The Director's Role in the Home–School Partnership

As a program leader, you are committed to including, valuing, and supporting *all* families. Without an inclusive view of families, a program community cannot thrive. Through the program's mission, vision, goals, and policies, you establish a culture for respectful, reciprocal home–school partnerships. Model forming and fostering these collaborative relationships with families and support teachers' efforts to do the same. Provide and promote plenty of opportunities for teachers and families to interact face to face outside of family conferences, including educational events, social gatherings, and home visits.

Directly from a Director

Start with an inclusive definition of *family*, like a circle of people who love and support you.

Getting to know more about families' values and cultures helps nurture the program's relationship with them, strengthens families' involvement and confidence in your staff and program, and enables children to be proud of their families and feel positive about their first school experiences. Institute activities for the whole center to participate in that encourage families to share their home culture with the program community. (See "Activities to Promote Family Engagement and Sharing" on the next page for a few ideas you can try.) These experiences often become cherished traditions of the program.

The Teacher's Role in the Home–School Partnership

In the classroom, teachers guide and inspire children to explore their similarities and differences as part of the curriculum. Effective teachers work hard to develop strong relationships and a cohesive engagement approach that encourages families to be active participants in the classroom community. Welcoming families into the classroom becomes a more personal experience since the teacher will know each child and his family on a deeper level than the director. The teacher should make sure families receive frequent information about their children's progress in the classroom as well as provide opportunities for families to share what children are doing at home. Families need to be able to interact with their child's teacher, and a single method of communication may not be universally accessible or convenient for everyone. Encourage teachers to use many different forms, like bulletin boards, class blogs and websites, newsletters, phone calls, emails, and in-person conversations, and to ask families which are the most effective for them.

Activities to Promote Family Engagement and Sharing

Family artifact bag

Provide each classroom with a cloth bag that zips or snaps shut to designate as a family artifact bag. Each class can decorate the bag if they like! Each child is given a turn during the year to take the bag home, where he and his family choose one or two things that are important and meaningful to them to place inside the bag—a recipe, photographs, a songbook. The next day, the child shares each item in the bag with the class and explains why it is special to his family. ("This is the recipe for the seafood pasta my grandma makes on Christmas Eve for the Feast of the Seven Fishes!") Encourage family members to come in and present to the class with their child (Derman-Sparks, LeeKeenan, & Nimmo 2015).

Family boxes

Ask each child in the program and her family to decorate the inside of a shoebox to represent their family. Provide some art materials for the children to take home and use, but keep the instructions open ended to allow each family to decorate the box however they choose. They may create a diorama or a collage with pictures clipped from magazines. When the boxes are complete, families bring them to the center so you and the teachers can create a collective display (Derman-Sparks, LeeKeenan, & Nimmo 2015).

Family photo project

Ask each child to take or choose five photos of their family that are meaningful to them. The photos can be taken with a family member's cell phone or with the classroom's disposable or digital camera if it can be sent home with children for an evening. The children share their photos with the rest of the class and explain why each one is meaningful to them. The photos can then be displayed around the classroom.

Funds of Knowledge Approach

Value families as experts with specific knowledge, practices, skills, and experiences that they pass on to their children. Having this viewpoint enables to you seek to learn *from* and *with* families rather than assuming the knowledge is all on your side to be imparted to families. This approach, known as *funds of knowledge*, is based on a concept developed by Moll and colleagues (1992), which reframes home–school relationships as partnerships where information is not transferred one way but exchanged reciprocally.

Having a better understanding of families' occupations and daily routines enables you and your staff to develop activities or projects that are connected to the children's lives. For example, if a child's family typically rubs her back to help her relax at bedtime, a teacher can use this same routine to help the child transition more easily to rest time. When the teacher incorporates home experiences with intentionality in the classroom, children are more emotionally secure and are more likely to take risks in learning because they feel safe and comfortable. Embracing this approach changes the following (Moll et al. 1992):

> **The nature of home visits.** Rather than see the home visit as an opportunity for teaching families what they think is best, teachers use the occasion to get to know and learn from the families.

> **The power structure of knowledge.** The teacher is not seen as the only one with specialized knowledge. Families have rich knowledge to share with teachers about their children and their family culture.

> **The child's sense of self.** Children feel empowered as learners when their families and teachers work together on their behalf.

When directors embrace and apply this strengths-based approach to their programs, the entire dynamic of early education settings shifts. The work of educating and caring for children becomes a collaborative effort between educators and families, and children experience a more harmonious connection between their homes and schools. Creating a program culture that allows for this equal exchange is hard work, but it is well worth the effort.

Welcoming Families to Your Program

Making families feel welcome is the first step to building home–school partnerships. This involves many small and not-so-small actions and activities, from sending emails that use intentionally inclusive language like "our" and "us" to strategically choosing art, photographs, books, and music that represent the diversity of the families served by your program. There are many ways directors can welcome and connect families in their program communities:

> During intake, give each family a welcome packet that includes a personal note.

> Post welcome signs in the home languages of the families in your program.

> Share information about program teachers by putting together a bulletin board with a photograph, job title, brief description, and fun fact for each.

> Create a display with a map, both teachers' and children's family photos, and the prompt "What cultures are part of your family?" Invite families and staff to mark the map with small dot stickers.

> Hold orientation meetings for families to learn more about the program policies, routines, and rituals and to solicit family ideas for engaging in the program.

> With permission, collect families' names, phone numbers, and email addresses, and compile a directory to share with all members of the program community.

> Establish a voluntary mentorship program where incoming families are paired with families whose children have been part of your program for some time. Mentor families can help new families get oriented and provide information and support.

You want a family's first one-on-one interaction with program staff to be positive, not due to a negative situation like a conference about their child's behavior. Make a conscious effort to create opportunities for pleasant first experiences. One director asks her teachers to call the family of each child in their class during the first month of school just to say hello, ask how their child is liking school so far, or share an anecdote about their child. The phone call is a just a brief check-in, but it's a positive one. When directors and teachers work to connect with each family from the start, if an issue or concern arises later, the foundation for a positive relationship has already been set.

Communicating with Families About the Program

While both educators and families need to be open to learning from each other, it is the program leader who sets the tone for reciprocal dialogue and learning (Derman-Sparks, LeeKeenan, & Nimmo 2015). Just as it is important for teachers to keep families informed about events in the classroom, it is equally important for directors to inform families about happenings in the school community at large. Communicate with families right from the start. As one director explains, "Starting off on the right foot can be simple, but it's critical. When families are dropping their children off in the morning, I like to check in and mention things like, 'Yesterday I popped into your son's classroom and observed him making the most amazing block structure! It included a road for cars and many buildings! Does he build complex structures like that at home?'" Initiating positive conversations can be joyful and engage families to be open to further conversations throughout the year.

There are a number of ways to keep families informed and to show your commitment and interest in them and their children. Be present at arrival and departure times, and meet and greet every family. Make the effort to get to know families personally and ask how things are going: "How do you like your new job? How is your mother feeling?" When families discuss something with you, employ active listening behaviors like nodding and maintaining eye contact.

The family handbook is another instrumental communication tool. It explains your program's philosophy, procedures, roles, schedules, and more, so make sure this document is clearly written and up to date. (For more on what to include in your family handbook, see Chapter 3.) Release your program calendar early so families can plan for vacations, staff professional development days, and school events and activities.

Write letters or newsletters for distribution to the entire program community, using a warm tone and inviting two-way communication. Include language that encourages families to respond, such as "We'd love to hear what children are saying about our centerwide focus on space exploration this week! Let us know by reaching out to us at . . ." Some directors write newsletters on a monthly basis; they can be distributed as hardcopies or sent via email. Regardless of the format, these letters should be easy to read and feature useful information, like program policy changes and updates, upcoming program events, and information about community events and resources.

Communicating with Families About Individual Learners

Arrival and departure transitions are among the most intense and stressful times in the program day. Families are trying to get to work, and teachers are trying to ease the transition between home and school. With emotions sometimes running high or families' thoughts elsewhere, families may have a difficult time receiving and processing information from a teacher about their child's school experiences. You might need to step in to help teachers think about how they communicate with families in these short, hectic windows of time.

Guide teachers to be intentional about the language and tone they use to speak with families. For example, rather than say, "Lea was very cranky today"—a statement that might make the family member feel defensive or guilty—the teacher should share this same information in a way that opens a conversation: "Lea seemed out of sorts today. It really helped her when she sat on my lap and we read a book together. Are there any strategies you use at home that work in situations like that?" By offering an explanation and inviting the family to participate in the dialogue, exchanges like this become a useful tool for families and teachers to pursue a common goal.

Depending on the staff scheduling in your program, the teacher who greets a child in the morning may not be the same one who sends him off at the end of the day. It's important that teachers always have something to share with a family about their child, even if they have only seen the child for the last hour of the day. One way to do this is for teachers to use written communication tools or systems for gathering and sharing information with each other and with families. Infant and toddler programs, for example, use a daily record sheet to note each child's eating, sleeping, and elimination schedules as well as her activities. Any teacher who works with a child that day can add to the sheet, and at the end of the day, the family has an account of their child's experiences. These record sheets may also include space for a family to write about their child's home experiences, such as his sleep schedule the night before, issues he might be experiencing like colic or diaper rash, and any other comments they may want to include. Similarly, two-way journals, where each child has a blank notebook that goes back and forth from home and school every day in their backpack, can foster better home–school communication. Families and teachers can use these notebooks to write short questions, comments, and observations about the child's day. Both of these tools not only encourage more free-flowing conversation between teachers and families about the children but also keep all the staff members who work with a child throughout the day informed by having all of the child's notes in one place.

In situations where families have limited English-language skills or basic reading and writing skills, a lengthy written account of the child's day may not work for their needs. Encourage teachers to be creative in their communication methods. A quick phone call or even a text to provide brief feedback might be preferable for some families. Most smartphones allow users to add multiple languages to their text messaging keyboards, and there are also apps that automatically translate text into other languages.

It is critical to schedule meetings and conferences at times and locations that are convenient for families. Opportunities for face-to-face interactions are essential to establish trust and exchange important information about children. While email should not be the sole or main avenue of communication between teachers and families, a more flexible policy might be necessary depending on the families' needs. It could be that a grandparent, extended family member, babysitter, or someone who is not the child's primary caregiver is regularly responsible for picking her up or dropping her off at school. In these cases, emails, texts, or phone calls might be the best available method to communicate with home.

Finally, help teachers understand how to speak with families about developmental behavior. Encourage them to avoid using professional jargon and use a good developmental checklist when communicating with families about which skills their child has and which the child is working on. (If your curriculum does not include a checklist that can be shared with families, there are a variety of excellent developmental checklists available online, such as the one offered by the Centers for Disease Control and Prevention at www.cdc.gov/ncbddd/actearly/milestones/index.html.) Programs can show families how to use the checklists as general guidelines to track their children's developmental successes and areas in need of support. Developing effective home–school communication takes time and effort. But the result is that you and the teachers will have a better relationship with the families of enrolled children, which ultimately helps your program serve the children better.

Using Technology to Communicate with Families

Technology allows educators and families to exchange information through websites, blogs, online messaging systems, emails, texting, social media, and online document sharing, just to name a few. Most schools have websites that sometimes include individual teacher or classroom webpages. These websites can be an important source of information for families and offer a quick way to connect with their child's teacher and classroom. On individual classroom websites, teachers typically include information such as upcoming events, initiatives, examples of classroom work, volunteer opportunities, and material requests. Directors should occasionally check individual classroom pages to ensure their quality and content. For working families who are unable to drop off or pick up their children in their classrooms or regularly attend program events, this can be an effective way to keep them connected to what's happening in their children's classrooms. While helpful, however, webpages take time to update, and teachers may need to remind families to look at them. The other challenge is that families must have access to web-enabled devices and an internet connection to view their child's class webpage.

While a program website usually contains general information that can be shared across all families (see pages 149–150 in Chapter 9 for more on program websites), information geared to specific children and families must be kept separate. For this reason, many school websites now have locked areas that are password accessible by individual families. Families need to sign permission forms to allow photographs of their children to be posted on the websites.

Social media and community engagement apps, such as SchoolCNXT and ClassDojo, can also provide new opportunities for communicating information. These apps offer a secure way to manage family contact lists and quickly share information. Some also offer live translation in multiple languages and text-to-speech to overcome communication barriers so all families can be included in teacher updates.

Work with teachers to help them determine what method of communication is appropriate for the information they want to share with the child's family. To ensure that technology is being used appropriately, you might provide more explicit guidance through policies in your program staff and family handbooks. While texts and emails are quick and efficient, they are best suited for informal communication, such as sending a photo of Jackson's in-progress art project. More formal information, like assessments or addressing a challenging behavior, is best shared in a face-to-face discussion that allows for two-way conversation and where body language, facial expressions, and tone provide more nuanced communication. That said, it is also important to consider each family's individual situation and use the communication strategy that works best for them. Perhaps Alicja's mother, who primarily speaks Polish and might struggle to follow a quick verbal update at departure time, would find it more helpful for the teacher to share photos that she has taken of Alicja throughout the day.

Directly from a Director

Technology has changed the face of communication, making everything faster and more accessible. That said, it should be used with care. Modern technology makes it very easy for families to contact teachers directly and at all hours. It was important for me, as director, to put a technology policy in place so families and staff could all be on the same page regarding what is appropriate and what is not.

Family Engagement

Directors who want their programs to collaborate successfully with families must be committed to doing more than sending an occasional newsletter or hosting a community event. Family engagement is much more demanding and multifaceted. It may be helpful to think of family engagement as occurring in the following categories (Epstein et al., forthcoming):

> **Parenting.** Help families support and nurture their children and add to their understanding and knowledge about their children and about child development.

> **Communicating.** Communicate with families about the program and their individual children through effective school-to-home and home-to-school communication methods.

> **Volunteering.** Improve recruitment, training, and schedules to involve families as volunteers and audiences at program activities and events.

> **Learning at home.** Help families extend their children's learning at home with curriculum-linked activities.

> **Decision making.** Include families as participants in program decisions and advocacy through boards, committees, and other family organizations.

> **Collaborating with the community.** Connect families with resources and services in the community and, in turn, partner with families to provide services to the community (e.g., a centerwide service day to beautify the local park).

Use this framework as a guide, and choose practices that will help achieve your specific program's goals and meet the needs of the children and families you serve.

Families differ in their life experiences, expectations of a program, and how they raise children, and programs need to accommodate these differences by providing a range of ways for families to be involved. Families will not take part in everything, but you "should try to offer some opportunities that mesh with their skills, energy, and availability" (Derman-Sparks, LeeKeenan, & Nimmo 2015, 71). Value all levels of engagement and contributions families make, from getting their child to school and ready for the day to being a member of the family advisory board. If it's within your program's means, you might provide child care during events to make it possible for more families to attend. Reach out and ask families how they would like to participate in their child's experiences at school; they may have ideas and suggestions you haven't considered.

Family Goals Sheet

A family goals sheet (like the one on page 133) is a concrete way to find out more about a family's values, beliefs, and strengths as well as their hopes and dreams for their child. This information can be gathered as part of the intake process, during a home visit, at family–teacher conferences, or even over the phone. Both program leaders and teachers can use the information provided to engage the family more fully in the program and to help support a family's goals for their child through the curriculum and center practices when possible.

Family Goals Sheet

Child's Name: _____   Date: _____

Name(s) of family member(s) completing the form: _____
_____

Name(s) of other important people in your child's life and their relationship to your child: _____
_____

What are your child's likes and dislikes? _____
_____

What are your child's strengths? _____
_____

What hopes, dreams, and goals do you have for your child at school this year? _____
_____

Please share any other information about your child and your family that you feel will help us understand your child better, including medical issues, culture, languages spoken, and family skills and traditions: _____
_____

Home Visits and Visits Outside of the Center

Home visits are an excellent way for teachers to learn about families in your program. Connecting with families outside the program setting can be less intimidating and more casual for some families. Some educators conduct home visits before a child begins the program to get to know the child better and help her feel more comfortable about transitioning to the program; however, visits can happen anytime during the year. It is important to explain the purpose of a visit to a family in advance. While it's a good idea to cover this aspect of your program in writing in your family handbook, share this information face to face as well, perhaps during family orientation. This provides families the opportunity to ask questions or learn more details. For example, a director might explain to a family during the intake process that their child's teacher will reach out soon to schedule a time to meet with them to better get to know them and their child and to allow them to get to know their child's teacher. At this time, you can also explain that this visit typically happens in the family's home so the teacher can observe the child in a familiar environment where she feels comfortable.

Some families may be apprehensive or reluctant about the idea of a home visit. They may worry about being judged or feel that the visit is an invasion of their privacy. As one parent expressed, "I was very nervous about the teacher coming to my home. I felt I had to clean the house and be sure everything looked nice. I was surprised how excited my child was to show the teacher her toys and where she slept. It was also nice to have some one-on-one time with the teacher in the privacy of my own home, so I could ask some more personal questions about the school."

Before these visits, directors should do what they can to help families feel at ease and create a relaxed atmosphere for when the teacher goes to visit. When visiting the home is not an option because a family does not wish it or for any other reason, visits can also take place in a space outside the family's home like a playground, nearby park, or even an area in the center that is not the child's classroom. Use of a neutral space can help families feel more comfortable and receptive to the idea. In cases where a family is completely against the idea of a home visit or a visit of any kind, even in a neutral space, to maintain a positive relationship it's best to respect the family's wishes.

Although home visits are typically brief, they have far-reaching impacts on the relationship between families and teachers. They can help

> Teachers understand more about the child's experiences outside of school

> Teachers learn about the family, their expectations and goals for their child, and resources and skills they may be able to offer your program

> Families feel more comfortable asking questions in their home setting or neutral space

> Ease the transition from home to school for children new to a group setting

Quick Tips for Effective Home Visits

 Be punctual and don't stay too long (a typical home visit lasts 30–45 minutes at most)

 Bring
- A family information packet and/or family goals form
- A toy or book from the center to show the child
- A digital camera to let the child take photos of things that are important to her to share with the class

 After the home visit, display photos from each child's visit in a class book, on a bulletin board, or above each child's cubby, with the family's permission

Teachers can also connect what they learn about a child and her family during a visit to new ideas and skills that are taught in the classroom throughout the year, as in the following vignette:

> Rory, a preschool teacher at Forest Grove Academy, smiles widely as the door to the Valente home swings open to reveal 4-year-old Ella and her father, Marco. After reintroducing herself briefly and thanking Marco for welcoming her into their home, Rory feels a light tug on her hand.
>
> Ella is jumping up and down excitedly. "Wait until you see what we've been making for you!"
>
> She leads Rory down the hall, where a wonderful smell is coming from. In the kitchen, Ella's mom, Azra, is pulling simit bread from the oven. The table is set with Ella's play tea things.
>
> Rory goes through the Forest Grove welcome packet with Marco and Azra, answering their questions and telling them more about the program and her classroom. She also asks Ella about what she likes to do and her favorite things to play with, taking mental notes to jot down Ella's responses later. During their conversation, Azra serves the simit bread, explaining how her mother in Turkey loved to make it and how they customarily serve it with tea.
>
> Later in the school year, Rory leads her class in a month-long study of bread, and she bring up her visit with Ella's family. "I cannot wait to learn about different types of bread with all of you. Ella, I remember how your family made some delicious simit bread to share with me when I came to visit. I hope you'll teach us all some things about simit bread."
>
> A huge smile spreads across Ella's face. She is so proud.

Family Meetings and Conferences

There are many different types of family meetings that occur in a program. They might be held between teachers and families or the director and families. Some are held in a group setting, such as when general informational updates need to be shared with everyone, while others might be one-on-one between an individual family and either the director or the teacher. The latter is more appropriate in situations where more personalized or confidential matters need to be discussed. No matter what kind of meeting is being held, the goal is always the same: to grow the relationship between the family and program through a reciprocal exchange of information and learning that will benefit everyone, including the child.

Meetings should not be reserved for only when there is a concern to be discussed. A conference, especially a one-on-one conference, is a prime stage to showcase what a child is learning in the classroom, emphasize her strengths and interests, share suggestions for how the family might extend her learning at home, and more. Share with a family what the meeting is about beforehand so they know what to expect. If there is a specific concern to be addressed, the program leader should meet with the classroom teacher to understand the situation so that everyone can be prepared to meet with the family. It is helpful to have the director present, for example, if the teacher needs to discuss a serious learning issue or behavioral challenge with the family or if there is a tense situation between two family members. More information about how to handle confrontations with families can be found on pages 138–141.

Building Community Through Family Events

Organizing community activities throughout the year is important to your efforts to foster camaraderie, spirit, and pride. These events can be social, educational, or fundraisers—sometimes all three! Your key purpose in planning these events is to create an opportunity for families to connect with other families. Ask families what events they would like to see and participate in, and incorporate their ideas into the plan for the year. Families can be great resources for each other, and by providing spaces where they can socialize, you help foster their sense of belonging and participation in the program community. Share the schedule of these events early in the year so families and staff can reserve the dates. The following are just a few examples of the kinds of events you can host, sponsor, organize, or even just encourage families and staff to attend as well as attend yourself.

Family fun time. Organize a centerwide hike or walk at a nearby park to encourage fitness and nature appreciation. Partner with a local family-friendly museum or concert venue to arrange a time for families to explore and enjoy together.

Food events. Meals are often a good way to bring people together. Potlucks allow everyone to participate in whatever way they can and alleviate the burden on the center of providing food for a crowd. Invite families to sign up to bring an appetizer, main course, side dish, dessert, or beverages. You might encourage families to also bring and share the recipe for their dish. Later, these recipes could be assembled into a cookbook and sold as a fundraising effort. Spaghetti nights are another possibility. Some programs have pasta, sauce, bread, and salad ingredients donated by local supermarkets and then charge families a small fee for the dinner.

Quick Tips for Effective Family Meetings

 Start by clarifying the goals of the meeting.
- What is the purpose of this meeting?
- What questions are you discussing?

 Schedule group meetings at a time that is convenient for most—ideally, all—families to attend. Be flexible in scheduling family–teacher conferences to accommodate individual family members' work hours and other commitments.

 Recognize that educators and families might have different feelings and expectations about conferences based on preconceived notions, previous experiences, or their own childhoods. These differences in perspective may lead to disagreements over things like behavior management strategies, communication, and developmental expectations. When disagreements occur, stop and check your own emotions about the situation or issue. They may also stem from cultural differences or an individual family's beliefs and values; whatever the cause, acknowledge and work through the differences.

 Remember that you are not delivering a monologue. A conference is a dialogue you and the family should participate in.
- Listen carefully so you can better understand the family's perspective.
- Avoid using educational jargon, and when necessary, arrange for an interpreter who speaks the family's home language.
- During meetings try to do more listening than talking—as the saying goes, you have one mouth but two ears!

 Know your limits. If a child has needs that you and your program are not equipped to handle, it is important to acknowledge that and to help families find the appropriate resources.

Family curriculum workshops. Curriculum workshops allow families to see firsthand some of what their children are learning. Organize a family literacy, math, or science afternoon (or evening) by setting up different centers, along with directions, for families to participate in curriculum activities with their children. Activities might include a bookmaking station, color mixing, and making patterns with construction paper shape cutouts.

Families' night out. Program staff can invite families to drop off their children for a few hours in the evening and provide child care for a flat fee. Families can enjoy the evening knowing their children are being well cared for by their teachers. This can be a great fundraiser.

Family interest and support groups. Many programs offer different types of interest and support groups for families. A director or teacher may be a facilitator, but families are also a support and resource for each other. Depending on your families' interests and needs, you might offer groups for single parents, multiracial families, families of children with disabilities, or families with adopted children. These groups could share recent articles or books of interest, watch films and have discussions, invite speakers, or share cultural activities.

Managing Confrontations, Conflicts, and Challenges with Families

Conflict is something many people want to avoid, but seasoned directors know that interpersonal challenges in a program setting are inevitable. While it is a difficult part of the job, situations that involve disagreement and tension offer opportunities for sharing and understanding others' perspectives. A facilitative leadership approach to conflict involves seeing it as an opportunity to find better resolutions.

Productive handling of differences in a program does *not* begin when an actual conflict occurs. Directors must work intentionally and proactively to create a culture and a climate in which disagreement is acceptable and constructive problem solving supports positive outcomes. It is also essential to recognize that there are no theoretical or perfect solutions. Some ambiguity and uncertainty is an inevitable part of this process. Rather, look for resolutions to specific conflict episodes that make sense in terms of your program's values and context (Derman-Sparks, LeeKeenan, & Nimmo 2015).

Derman-Sparks, LeeKeenan, & Nimmo (2015) recommend a problem-solving technique called *finding the third space*, which involves three steps that encourage the conflicting parties to communicate openly and honestly to reach a compromise:

Step 1: Acknowledge. Analyze the situation. Recognize that there is a difference in opinions, belief, or values that needs to be addressed. Avoid becoming defensive or rushing to judgment.

Step 2: Ask. Gather information from all parties that will contribute to understanding the underlying issues. Find out what the issue means to the family and what the family would do or has done in the past. Clarify the priorities and be open to the need to learn.

Step 3: Adapt. Taking into account the information gathered in step 2, think of ways to adapt policies and practices in the center. Find common ground and consider alternatives. Identify and be straightforward about nonnegotiable values and practices.

The following sections illustrate how finding the third space can be applied in two kinds of conflicts. The first is a conflict between program staff and a family, and the second explores a situation where the program is put in the middle of a conflict between family members.

Conflict Between Program Staff and Families

Mei-lan is 3½ years old and new to the preschool program. When it is snack and lunchtime, her teacher, Simona, notices that she does not show any interest in her food and makes no attempt to eat. After this happens two days in a row, when Mei-lan's parents arrive to pick her up at the end of the day, Simona mentions that she has not been eating her lunch and snack.

Mei-lan's parents are confused. "Why don't you feed her?" they ask.

Now it is Simona's turn to be confused. When she explains that the program encourages children to feed themselves at this age, the parents become upset and concerned. They insist that Simona should feed their daughter since that's what she's used to at home and what is typical in their family culture. Simona is unsure of what to do and decides to bring this situation to the attention of the program director, Cleo.

Step 1: Acknowledge

Cleo and Simona recognize that a conflict exists: Mei-lan's family and the program have different expectations about mealtime behavior, and Mei-lan is caught in the middle. Mei-lan's parents see feeding their child as a way to show love and care. The program expects more autonomy and independence for a child at this age, and there is not enough staff to feed each child.

Step 2: Ask

Cleo and Simona talk with the family about Mei-lan's eating habits and clarify the program's beliefs and priorities in the situation. Cleo also facilitates conversations between the family and Simona with the goal of understanding where each side stands on the issue and their desired outcome.

Step 3: Adapt

Together, Cleo, Simona, and Mei-lan's parents look for common ground and consider alternative ways to solve the problem. Cleo might suggest to Simona that in some cases, in order to maintain positive relationships with families and accommodate an individual child's need, it is acceptable to use different strategies with different children. Ultimately, the family provides some finger foods Mei-lan can eat by herself and Simona has one of the assistant teachers sit next to Mei-lan at mealtimes to help support her growth toward independence. "Understanding different cultural practices does not require determining which one way is 'right'. . . . With an understanding of what is done in different circumstances, we can be open to possibilities that do not necessarily exclude each other. . . . There is *always* more to learn" (Rogoff 2003, 14).

Ideally, your family handbook should include procedures for negotiating differences of opinion and conflicts that arise between your families and program staff. The first step is for the two parties who disagree, typically a family and their child's teacher, to try to negotiate the conflict. If a compromise or agreement cannot be reached, then the director should be involved. If a satisfactory resolution still cannot be achieved with the director, then a family might meet with the director's overseeing body—a board or the executive director. Families can also appeal to the program's licensing agency or another quality assurance body.

Conflict Between Family Members in the Context of the Program

Asha, the director of a preschool program, always leaves her office door open as families arrive to drop off and pick up their children so they know she's available to them. As she works at her desk one afternoon, she hears a knock and looks up to find the father of 3-year-old Hayden, looking quite flustered.

In a gruff voice, he says, "Can I speak with you?"

Asha smiles and offers him a seat.

"You see, it just can't happen anymore. I don't want my ex-wife's boyfriend picking up my son again. I don't agree with it, I don't like it, and it's not right."

Asha is caught off guard. She can see that Hayden's father is worried, upset, and even a little angry, but this is a situation she's unsure how to respond to.

Step 1: Acknowledge

Asha realizes there is a difference of opinion between Hayden's father and his ex-wife, Hayden's mother. There are clearly high emotions at play, and she realizes that there needs to be a meeting with all interested parties.

Step 2: Ask

Asha requests a meeting with Hayden's father and mother to discuss a pickup schedule. She asks them to clarify who picks up Hayden on which days. Hayden's mother has a conflict on one of her days, Wednesday, over the next few months due to her class schedule for the semester. Because of this, she had asked her new boyfriend to pick up Hayden on those days. While the program was informed, it's clear that this is new information for Hayden's father.

Step 3: Adapt

Asha suggests the two parents come up with an agreed-upon solution for pickup and let the program know the plan in writing, including whether the schedule is permanent or just for the rest of the semester.

What do you do when there are challenges between teachers and families or between family members? When there are challenges between teachers and families or between family members, you might be able to find a way to support communication between the parties with limited guidance. Or, like Cleo and Asha, you may find it necessary to step in and mediate the situation. When challenging topics need to be addressed, offering support and facilitating conversation can help ease the path to resolution. When appropriate, document the issues in a follow-up letter to families, outlining what was discussed and what resolutions the program and the families agreed upon. It's important that the child's family doesn't feel that program staff are all working against them, and input from a party not directly involved in the conflict can provide the perspective needed to problem solve amicably and effectively. Active listening throughout the discussion process is vital to resolving conflict.

As you can see, working with families is not a one-time effort to check off your list. It is an ongoing process, one that needs continual time, attention, and commitment from you and your staff. The most important component of a home–school partnership is building respectful and trusting relationships between educators and families. Finding opportunities for two-way communication with families, providing mutual support for teachers and families, and empowering families to be a vital part of their children's education are all valuable undertakings for a vibrant, successful program.

Big-Picture Takeaways

> Families' roles as their children's first teachers cannot be underestimated. Robust home–school partnerships are built on the understanding that educators learn about children from and with families.

> Use a wide range of ways to communicate with families. One size does not fit all.

> Do not shy away from conflict. Interpersonal challenges in a program setting are inevitable and should be seen as opportunities to find common ground, compromise, and work toward resolution when possible.

Go Deeper

Creating Welcoming Schools: A Practical Guide to Home–School Partnerships with Diverse Families, by J. Allen (Teachers College Press; International Reading Association, 2007)

"Principles of Family Engagement": NAEYC.org/resources/topics/family -engagement/principles

Welcoming Schools, A Project of the Human Rights Campaign Foundation: www.welcomingschools.org

Chapter Nine

>> Center Enrollment

Many a small thing has been made
large by the right kind of advertising.

—Mark Twain, *A Connecticut Yankee in King Arthur's Court*

The goal for all centers is near-full to full enrollment. When a center is not operating at capacity, it is difficult to be financially successful and to offer a high-quality program that meets the needs of children, families, and the community. Many directors have little or no training in advertising or business promotion, and full enrollment can be a daunting task. Implementing an effective recruitment and enrollment plan involves understanding your program's unique strengths and attributes and how they fulfill the needs of the community—and communicating this to potential families.

Your program might be affiliated with a larger umbrella organization—such as a corporation, social service agency, religious community, or university—that supports your efforts to reach out to families and enroll children. If you direct an independent program, however, you are probably responsible for organizing and executing your own plan for marketing, admissions, and enrollment. Here are a few initial points to consider:

> What population does your program serve?

> What kind of demand is there for the offerings of your program?

> Who is your competition?

> What is your program's reputation?

> How do prospective families find out about your program?

Some centers are based in neighborhoods where early childhood education is in high demand with little competition; other programs compete against many early childhood education options in their area and actively recruit families with young children. Centers with Head Start services, sliding scale fees, or federal funding that serve families with low income must follow regulatory considerations. In these cases, directors will make this aspect of their program known through focused efforts to recruit eligible families and partner with local organizations that serve their target population. Whatever situation applies to your program, marketing is crucial to generating continued visibility and interest in your program to keep enrollment up, both now and in the future.

Marketing, Advertising, and Recruiting

Market Research

Before launching your program—and even after it's established, if you're considering changing your services or you need to get a handle on why enrollment is decreasing—it is imperative that you conduct market research. Market research is a way of collecting information you can use to determine a population's needs and interests to inform, better shape, and promote your program's services. One director explained, "I didn't realize that in most families in my town, the parents work full time. This meant that my original

idea of running a half-day program wasn't going to be successful. Families in my neighborhood needed full-time care. If I hadn't researched the market prior to advertising my program, no one would have come to my school! It would have been a huge mistake." Thorough market research will also help you avoid such mistakes as well as help you create a program identity that resonates with the community you wish to serve and differentiates it from other programs in the area. Starting any business is challenging, and it is important to learn about prospective clients and existing demands and needs in the area.

"At first," another director told us, "I was hesitant to spend some of my budget on market research. I just figured if I opened a beautiful program, the clients would come. This was not true at all. Market research helped me identify and prepare for the community my business would be existing in. I avoided a lot of mistakes." Some directors take on market research themselves while others hire consultants to help them. You can use the library, internet, and other sources like town demographic records and city or state education department meetings to help you learn as much as you can about your area and the education values and challenges it holds. This will help you improve and position your program for success.

Spend time learning about other programs in the area, including the range of services they provide, hours, tuition rates, enrollment capacity, philosophy, teacher training, and facilities. State and local child care resource and referral agencies often have lists of licensed programs and centers available for free or a small fee. As the availability of public pre-K programs increases, private programs serving preschool children must find out how many preschoolers are being served in the community by the public school system. This can hugely affect the feasibility of a private program, as providing care to preschoolers is more profitable than serving infants and toddlers due to necessary teacher–child ratios. If you cannot fill preschool classrooms due to broadly available public pre-K programs, your program may not be able to thrive. All of this information will help you find your target market and price your services appropriately. Will your program be more or less expensive than other programs in the area, and why? How will you inform families about the value of your program's services? How is your program different than others offered close by? Answering these questions is critical to effectively advertise your program.

Be Clear About Your Program's Mission, Philosophy, and Services

It is impossible to sell something unless it is clear what you offer and what makes those services stand out from the competition. Once you've researched the market of prospective families in the community, focus on promoting the qualities your program has that fulfill their needs and wants. What is your program philosophy? Is it a bilingual program? Does it focus on a particular area, like math or technology? Does it have a unique outdoor learning environment? Is it known for a garden that the children tend? Does it have a low teacher–child ratio? Do you have a high percentage of degreed and experienced teachers? Is the program connected to a research institution or partner with other programs in the community? Does it offer before- or after-school programs? Are grandparents or students invited to volunteer regularly? Is there a family engagement and/or education component? Does the program have a special emphasis on diversity and inclusion? Does your program provide lunch and snacks, supply diapers, or offer transportation or other services to ease family life? Are evening or weekend hours available? In your center's promotional materials, highlight whatever services or features make your program special.

Everyone involved in the recruitment, enrollment, and admissions process must be able to describe and discuss the unique aspects of your program in an informed way. With your staff, discuss the aspects everyone feels deserve marked promotion, and make sure all of you are on the same page regarding the program identity and selling points. For example, when you or the staff talk to prospective families, do you want to emphasize the program's play-based nature or its focus on literacy? Maybe you want to tie them both together. Work with your staff to develop a statement of goals for the program, which can be a list of the program's best selling points and strengths. One might be, for example, "We strive to provide a play-based environment that encourages children to learn by doing." Staff engagement not only helps build your program community but also goes a long way toward marketing your program.

Some directors even create an *elevator speech,* or a clear, succinct message about the program, with their staff so that everyone can deliver a strong, unified description about what is unique about your program and why it's a great place for families in just a few sentences.

Marketing Tools and Avenues

Once you've identified your key audience and your selling points that will help fill their needs, it's time to let families know about your program and its value. From flyers to social media to your website, anything you put out there for potential families to see should be designed carefully and thoughtfully represent your program goals and services. The possibilities for how to promote your program are broad, and it may take some trial and error before finding the combination that is most effective for you. The following are just a few of the approaches you can explore.

Physical Visibility

Physical visibility and appeal of your program can be an important marketing tool. Keep a well-maintained sign that is easily read from the road so that people passing by notice your program. Many cities have rules about signage, so be sure to have approval before you post anything. Often, families need programs that are close to their home or on their commute to work, so catching their eye with prominent, attractive signage goes a long way in drawing their attention and interest. In addition, keep the exterior of your program tidy and beautiful—fresh paint, vibrant flower beds, and general curb appeal—so that potential families will be attracted to the space.

Open Houses and School Tours

Often, the best way to show prospective families that your program is the right fit for their children is by inviting them to observe and learn more about it in person. Many programs offer open houses once or twice a year. Depending on whether you operate a year-round program or one from fall to spring, the timing of the open houses may vary. School-year programs tend to offer an open house in the fall, while year-round programs might offer one in the fall and one in the spring. Some programs keep their open house informal, inviting families to speak with teachers if they have questions and freely explore classroom and playground spaces. Other programs find it helpful to have a more structured approach. You might limit attendance to adult family members only and format it as more of a guided tour or discussion. Or, you can draw interested families by framing your open house as a community event, like a musical performance, a puppet show, or a book sale. During open houses, be present in a central location to greet all visiting families and answer questions.

Programs also offer school tours to interested families throughout the school year. These tours often include a group meeting with the director and a walk around the center with an opportunity to peek in the classrooms. In the meeting, the director will emphasize the program's philosophy and goals and answer any questions families might have. Let families know if children are welcome to come or if tours are intended only for adults. While families should be able to observe the program in action, it is important to minimize distractions for children and teachers in the classrooms. Consider scheduling prospective visits for adult family members at any time but reserving visiting hours with children for after-school hours or on weekends. Some programs are fortunate enough to have windows so that families can see into the classrooms without disturbing the children. If a tour group enters a classroom, families should understand where to sit and walk. Inside a classroom, families should be quiet and reserve conversation for outside the classroom. There are some cases where it's important to observe a prospective child with other children; in these situations, you can work with teachers to find the appropriate, least disruptive time to have the child visit, such as during choice time or group time.

Whenever prospective families are visiting, have written materials about the program available, such as brochures, applications, information about tuition and fees, and a general introduction to the program's philosophy and schedule. For a more personalized experience, use nametags for visitors and teachers. Beverages and snacks also help create a friendly atmosphere, and be sure to have plenty of age-appropriate, hands-on activities for visiting children.

Print Collateral

Print marketing materials, including brochures, flyers, and newsletters, are versatile, cost-effective promotional tools. While print collateral can vary in length, much like with an elevator speech, your goal is to convey key information and tout the best qualities of your program succinctly and in a way that makes people want to know more. There is, of course, the added dimension of being visually engaging. Be thoughtful about clean layouts that flow sequentially and are not too cluttered or distracting. Think about both the language you use as well as the images you feature. If your program has a logo, which is recommended, it should both represent your program and stand out from other logos of early childhood education centers in the area. Photographs and images should be high quality, be representative of your program, and enhance your message, not distract from it. Above all, be sure to prominently include your program's contact information—physical address, phone number, email, website URL, and social media handles.

Once you have these marketing pieces ready, consider how you can distribute them and make them accessible. If you have access to mailing lists with your population demographic, direct mail is a useful strategy. Some programs ask families, staff, and community service volunteers to deliver flyers and center brochures door to door. You might also place written material in public spaces or other locations frequented by families in the community, like libraries, grocery stores, places of worship, pediatric offices, parks, and coffee shops. Ask local businesses to display a program flyer in their windows. Many communities also have public bulletin boards at libraries and at the town hall.

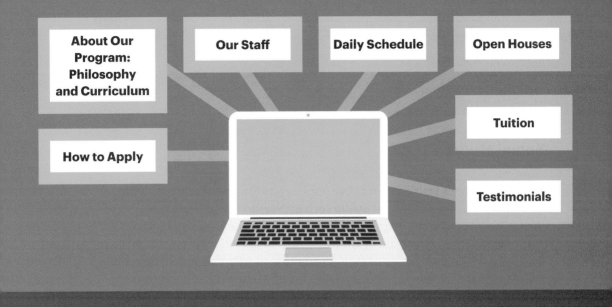

Sample Program Website Navigation

About Our Program: Philosophy and Curriculum

Our Staff

Daily Schedule

Open Houses

Tuition

How to Apply

Testimonials

Website

Businesses of all types need an online presence for visibility, sharing information, and advertising. For many communities, online advertising proves to be more efficient than traditional methods of advertising. When possible, include technology support and website design in your budget or seek out a volunteer from your program or local community to help with the website.

Directly from a Director

Our website is the most critical piece of our school's promotional materials. Most families apply online and email us questions using the contact form.

As you create or improve your website, solicit and consider feedback from colleagues and your center's staff, families, and community about the various elements of your website, including the following:

> **Text.** Is the font type and color easy to read? Is the language used to describe your program concise, understandable, and engaging? Are there typos?

> **Images.** High-quality, interesting photos make a website feel more personal, and prospective families find it very helpful to see images of a program's interior and exterior learning spaces. (Keep in mind that if you use images of the children enrolled in your center on the website, families must give written permission.)

> **Content.** Is the information available on your website an accurate, up-to-date representation of your program (e.g., mission, facilities, current staff)?

> **Ease of navigability.** The organization and design should make finding the information on your website an intuitive process. See "Sample Program Website Navigation" on page 149 for an example of sections your website might contain.

> **Accessibility.** Is the information on your site available in multiple languages, as needed by the population of the community you serve? Does your website adhere to accessibility guidelines for people with disabilities, such as visual and hearing impairments?

Social Media

Creating a presence on social media is another effective way to share information about your program. Use public platforms like Facebook, Twitter, and Instagram and local social media such as Nextdoor to provide basic information about your program and announce open houses, school tours, fundraising events, hiring opportunities, program activities, interesting class field trips, new initiatives, and more. In addition to giving staff, families, and members of the community another stage on which to interact and engage, these sites allow users to follow, like, and share content you post with friends and relatives, organically generating traffic to your pages. Here are a few general tips for using social media in this context:

> When possible, include links to relevant pages on your website in posts.

> Try to engage with users who comment on your posts, whether you reply directly or like or share their comment as the situation and platform warrant.

> Use platforms as they are intended to be used. On Instagram, post original images and videos rather than text-heavy posts. Keep Tweets short.

Even with great content, it can take time to build up a following on social media. If you have money in your marketing budget, consider paid options to optimize your advertising reach. For example, Facebook allows you to pay a fixed amount of money to *boost,* or more widely promote, a specific post to a wider audience on the platform based on their location, age, gender, and interests. When interested families contact you, ask how they found you. Over time, you'll develop a sense of what platforms your families use and value. While these social media habits will shift over time, this information can help guide your efforts.

Word of Mouth

When all is said and done, no brochure, website, or newspaper advertisement can take the place of word of mouth. Families with children currently enrolled in your program are your most powerful asset in finding and connecting with new families. Talk with current families about their experience in your program, including what has made it positive for them and what they feel could be improved. Ask families and staff to write testimonials for the center's promotional materials. Update testimonials frequently to keep them fresh and current. Some programs even offer referral bonuses when current families recruit new families to enroll. Prospective families often appreciate the opportunity to speak directly with current families about their experiences in the program. Find a few representatives from each classroom who are willing to talk with interested families by email or phone.

Directly from a Director

Word of mouth is everything. If you run a good program, people will talk about it and you will have less trouble filling slots! But your work does not stop there; you need to keep improving and demonstrating why your program is a positive learning environment for children.

More Ideas

> **Ads in newspapers.** While placing an advertisement in a larger national newspaper can be expensive, local or regional newspapers and newsletters are often a more cost-effective and successful route. Some larger corporate early childhood programs rely on national advertisements to build their brand, but most small programs rely on local newspapers to reach clients directly.

> **Ads in association publications.** If you run a larger or newly established program, advertising in larger early childhood education publications like *Young Children, Exchange Magazine,* and *Education Week* can be effective. These publications often feature early education products and services and include interesting stories about new businesses in the industry.

> **Local networking.** Most towns and cities have community events, such as early childhood education fairs, where you, staff, or family members of children enrolled in your program can talk with attendees who are interested in learning about the programs in the area. Create a display that highlights your program, distribute marketing collateral, or sponsor activities like a crafts table or read-alouds to get your program's name out there.

> **Education workshops.** Organize a single workshop or workshop series for prospective families. The focus of your workshop should be a topic that reflects the expertise of you and your staff and that interests families, such as addressing challenging toddler behaviors or learning activities they can do at home with their preschoolers. Look for local family–child groups willing to have you come and speak on a topic of interest to them. Have marketing materials available for families to take with them.

> **Free publicity.** Local media outlets, from newspapers to television and radio stations, are always on the lookout for interesting stories. Why not your program? Research some of the channels to see what kind of stories they want and what their requirements are. Is your center raising funds to purchase goats for a community in need? Or perhaps children are learning how to make pizza from a local restaurant? Let an outlet know what you are doing! A simple article about your program can be of interest to many. In some cases, the newspaper will invite you to write and submit an article for consideration; in other cases, they will send a reporter to interview you, staff, and the children to create a broadcast or write an article.

> **Listservs.** Find out if your local community has a *listserv,* a specialized email group people with a shared interest can subscribe to and receive messages. There may be listservs for general community information, families new to the area, or those specifically with young children or interested in education.

Application and Admissions Process

Application Materials

Your program's application is an opportunity to collect information about families who are interested in joining your school community. Make sure your application captures the demographic information you need and asks thoughtful questions about a family's educational goals for their child.

The application may be a family's first connection with your program. What you include in the application and how you ask the questions reflect the program's values. The wording, organization, and even formatting of the document will lead families to form an impression of what the program experience will be like. Is it organized and tidy? Does it use inclusive language that welcomes all types of learners? Be thoughtful about this document and be sure it represents the underlying philosophy of your program.

Your program's application should be easy to fill out. In some communities, it might need to be translated into other languages. The following is a suggested layout for an application packet:

1. The **instruction page** invites the family to apply to your program. It should clearly and concisely state the process families need to follow to enter the program, including important deadlines.

2. A **guarantee of confidentiality** should preface any request for information. Assure families that any information they provide will be kept private and will not be disclosed to anyone beyond the program director, the admission committee, and/or the child's teacher.

3. The **program application form** collects all basic information about the child, including his full name, date of birth, and gender, as well as information about his family. Use language that is inclusive of diverse family structures; instead of *mother* and *father,* use a more open-ended term like *family* with plenty of space for the responses to accommodate and respect all families. Other information that's useful to collect includes

> ❭ Sibling information, including birth order and if there are younger siblings

> ❭ Any prior applications for the child's admittance into the program

4. The **background information section** invites families to share information about their cultural, ethnic, religious, and family backgrounds that they feel is important for the program to know to provide their child with positive, nurturing experiences. Is the child a dual language learner? If so, what is her home language? Who are the important adults in this child's life? Does the child live with extended family where her grandparents or other people have a major role in her care? What holidays does the child celebrate?

5. **Family questions** invite the family to write about the child's interests, challenges, or needs. Leave plenty of space for families to share this information.

Family Interviews

As part of the application process, it is common to meet with the family in person to discuss their child and to determine if your program is a good fit for their child. It may take the form of an open-ended discussion or a more formal family interview. This face-to-face meeting gives you an opportunity to ask families questions and allows families to learn about the center. Here are some questions to consider including as part of this step:

1. What are you looking for in an early childhood setting?

2. What are some things your child loves to do?

3. How would you like to be involved in your child's learning experience?

4. What kind of teacher would you like for your child?

5. What are you most excited about as your child begins school?

6. What are you most concerned about as your child begins school?

7. Is there anything else you would like to share with us about your child?

Admissions and Selection

Programs conduct their admissions and selection process in many different ways. Some centers accept applications and admit children during a fixed window of time just once a year (or once a semester); other programs accept children as they apply and there is availability. Still others move families through an interview process followed by a committee selection. Regardless of how your program enrolls families, give careful thought to the process and clearly communicate each step to families.

A rolling admissions policy, in which the program considers and admits children as they apply, is common and has both advantages and disadvantages that require careful consideration. Continually accepting and reviewing applications can be time consuming. With rolling admission also comes the challenge of ensuring that your classrooms have enough tuition income to pay the bills. Because families can arrive at different times of the year, you will need to consider how much income upfront keeps your budget healthy and out of the red and, based on that information, determine how frequently to invoice families. Rolling admissions also potentially disrupts classroom stability. When the makeup of the classroom remains relatively consistent, on the other hand, children are more likely to develop close relationships. There are advantages to a rolling admissions policy as well. Families like that they do not have to wait for a specific window of time to find early child education and care. If a family experiences a job relocation or other circumstance that results in a child leaving your program unexpectedly, you will hopefully have a ready supply of pending or waitlisted applicants available to fill that opening quickly.

Regardless of your admissions and selection process, maintaining a waitlist for your program provides a ready lineup of potential children to enroll in your program as openings become available. Most directors use their waitlist with some discretion. For example, siblings of children who are already enrolled in your program may be given priority over others who are waiting. In programs that are part of a larger umbrella organization, such as a law firm or government agency, children of families who are employees of that organization might be given priority over children and families outside of the organization.

Notification of Acceptance and Intake Forms

When a child is accepted into your program, there are a number of documents you will need to provide to the family, including the following:

> A **welcome letter** is one of your first chances to communicate with the family. It should be warm and positive in tone and include highlighted dates for upcoming enrollment forms and deadlines. Provide information for families to connect with you via phone or email.

> A **tuition agreement** outlines the expected tuition payment schedule as well as penalties for late payment. This agreement is a binding document that families need to sign to acknowledge their agreement. To emphasize the commitment the family is making by enrolling their child in your program, you might consider requiring payment for the first few months of tuition upfront if possible. This will, of course, depend on whether this is a realistic expectation for the families and community you serve.

> A **family handbook** helps ensure that both the family and the program are on the same page regarding policies, procedures, and expectations. Consider including a statement that families sign to acknowledge that they have read, understand, and agree to the information it outlines.

> **Health forms** ask families to list allergies, immunizations, food restrictions, medication regimens, or other vital information program staff need to know to keep their children safe and healthy.

Directly from a Director

We used to charge tuition each month, but we had a lot of families not taking their slots seriously, dropping in and out of our program. It made accounting—and our classrooms—a mess. We moved to having tuition payments due on a quarterly basis, and since then, we have noticed that families take their children's enrollment in our program more seriously. Ultimately, I think it has helped our school community both fiscally and emotionally.

These documents should be kept organized in the children's files for easy access for future reference or in case of possible emergencies and inspections. Check children's health records to make sure all immunizations are up to date. Either the director or another staff member should alert families when their paperwork is expiring (e.g., enrollment and tuition agreements, food program contracts, medical forms) and ensure that the new paperwork is filled out and processed.

Almost everything a director does is in some way related to recruitment and keeping enrollment up. With strategic research and planning, you can make your program and its value visible to families in the community you serve.

Big-Picture Takeaways

> Before advertising your program, conduct market research to determine what needs in the community your services fulfill. This will be the key to your marketing and recruitment efforts.

> Consider the different tools you can use to market your program, including open houses, print collateral, a website, and social media. Find the combination that works best to reach the families in your community effectively.

> Make sure your application materials and process are straightforward, well organized, and transparent for families.

Go Deeper

Child Care Aware of America: www.childcareaware.org/providers

Child Care Marketing Solutions (CCMS): www.childcare-marketing.com

The Ultimate Child Care Marketing Guide: Tactics, Tools, and Strategies for Success, by K. Murray (Redleaf Press, 2012)

>> **Balancing Act—
Managing Your Role
as the Director**

A journey of a thousand miles begins
with a single step.

—**Lao Tzu,** *Tao Te Ching*

It is clear that being an effective director means skillfully striking the right balance between competing demands to keep your early childhood education program running successfully and smoothly. We would like to leave you with seven principles to guide your work.

Principle 1

Manage Your Time . . . and Appreciate Its Returns

Set concrete, realistic short- and long-term goals, both personal and professional. Write them down, review them periodically, and adjust them as needed. Whether it's your daily, quarterly, or annual to-do list, establish an order of priority and specific time limits for each task to help you avoid procrastination. Don't think of time as only an obstacle or a limitation. As time passes, you gain experience and reap the benefits of the observations, reflections, and relationships you've built.

Principle 2

Learn to Let Go

You are in this role because you know how to do many things well. You might even be a perfectionist, always willing to spend that additional hour or day or week to make that report better, improve that welcome bulletin board in the entryway, or plan for that staff meeting. But in a position with many and varied demands, an all-or-nothing mentality can be detrimental. Distinguish between *expectations* and *requirements*—these are not the same, and often your self-imposed expectations are far above what is actually needed. It's important to be able to recognize when what you've done is "good enough" for its purpose and move on to the next task rather than sink valuable time into making it flawless. In this, as with many things, you are a role model for your teachers and staff. You have the opportunity to set an example of moderation.

Another related skill of an effective leader is the ability to recognize that you can't do everything yourself. You need to know when to say "no more" and when to delegate. It can be hard to turn down a request from a teacher, a parent, or the board and feel as though you're disappointing them, but giving yourself permission to say no when you know you can't take on more is ultimately best for you and for your program. Often, it is more efficient and effective to complement your skills with your staff's. Identify staff members' strengths and share responsibilities with them wisely.

Sometimes, it's easy to focus on the challenges of being a director and forget about the joys. I try to remember that every day is a privilege where I get to help children, families, and teachers.

Principle 3
Exercise "Rotated Neglect"

It is your responsibility to keep all the aspects of your job in focus while recognizing that you can't do everything at once. As a director, Debbie frequently found it helpful to practice *rotated neglect*—putting some tasks on the backburner while dedicating time and attention to others, making sure to switch these out occasionally. As long as the same project is not being repeatedly neglected each day, each week, each month, you can find some balance and get things accomplished. Set small, short-term goals within the scope of larger, long-term undertakings. Identify what can be done today and what will be done another day.

Principle 4
Make Time for Self-Care

A director's job involves caring for and about others—children, families, staff, board members, the community, and other program constituents. You are so busy caring for others and putting their needs first that the most common thing you neglect is yourself. Be sure to incorporate self-care into your routine, whether that means exercising, getting some fresh air, reading a book not related to your job, or meeting a friend for lunch. Make a point to carve out time in your schedule so you can be recharged and refreshed before you tackle your work again. It's just as important to pencil in "go to the gym" or "take a five-minute music break" on your to-do list as "call the licensor" and "write the annual report." You might feel guilty taking time to do something for yourself, but balancing work with your personal well-being and having a bit of leisure time in your waking hours is essential to managing stress and avoiding burnout. When you take care of yourself, you are better able to take care of others.

Principle 5 — Be a Lifelong Learner

Being the best educator you can be means recognizing that your own growth and learning are never done. Just as it is a priority to support your staff's professional development, you also need to support your own. You always need to be extending your learning, feeding your passions and wonderings, and keeping current on the latest research, best practices, and tools in early childhood. Here are a few ways to be a more engaged, effective lifelong learner:

> Subscribe to print or digital journals.
> Visit and observe other early childhood programs and invite other early childhood leaders and teachers to visit your program. This is an opportunity to get feedback and share ideas.
> Attend a lecture, webinar, or workshop on a topic that excites you—or something you know nothing about!
> Take a course at a local community college or university, either online or face to face.
> Attend national conferences, such as NAEYC's Annual Conference or Professional Learning Institute and the McCormick Center for Early Childhood Leadership's Leadership Connections National Conference.

Principle 6 — Network

Being a director can be a lonely job. Typically, early childhood leaders are so busy at their own center that they do not reach out to find other directors and administrators in similar roles. Networking can be one of the best ways to find support, share ideas and tips, and problem solve issues. Start small by getting together on a monthly basis with a few other program leaders in your community to share ideas. These can be directors you already know, met at a conference, or even just reached out to via an email blast to local centers to arrange a meet-up. Director groups can be self-organized or have a paid facilitator. In some communities, director groups are formed by the local community organizations, including early childhood councils, child care resource and referral agencies, or other community partnerships.

Principle 7 — Be an Intentional Decision Maker

You may not always have the resources you need or want at your disposal, but you do have a vision, goals, and the power of your position to make decisions that move your program forward. Your decisions about curriculum, budgeting, hiring staff, and engaging families are not haphazard and neither are their outcomes. Be strategic, and always know the rationale behind the what, why, when, and how of what you do. It is easy to lose sight of the long view when you are mired in day-to-day tasks. Taking a step back from details and pausing to reflect on larger picture will help your decisions and actions be more purposeful.

With any journey, the path can seem long and the destination far, but it just takes one step to move forward. We hope that with the information and strategies in this book, your journey will be more easily navigated. Along the way, don't forget to appreciate the small steps—the impact you have every day with each child, family, and staff interaction. Your leadership does have an impact and does make a difference.

References

American Montessori Society. 2018. "Core Components of Montessori Education." Accessed April 28. www.amshq.org/Montessori-Education/Introduction-to-Montessori/Core-Components-of-Montessori-Education.

Angier, N. 2013. "The Changing American Family." *New York Times,* November 25. www.nytimes.com/2013/11/26/health/families.html.

Anitha, J. 2014. "Determinants of Employee Engagement and Their Impact on Employee Performance." *International Journal of Productivity and Performance Management* 63 (3): 308–23.

Artz, B. 2013. "The Impact of Supervisor Age on Employee Job Satisfaction." *Applied Economics Letters* 20 (14): 1340–43.

Bagnato, S.J., J.T. Neisworth, & K. Pretti-Frontczak. 2010. *LINKing Authentic Assessment and Early Childhood Intervention: Best Measures for Best Practices.* 2nd ed. Baltimore: Brookes Publishing.

Beesley, C. 2016. "How to Fire an Employee and Stay within the Law." *US Small Business Administration: Managing a Business* (blog). Last modified September 19. www.sba.gov/blogs/how-fire-employee-and-stay-within-law.

Bloom, P.J. 2014. *Leadership in Action: How Effective Leaders Get Things Done.* 2nd ed. Lake Forest, IL: New Horizons.

Bloom, P.J. 2016. *Measuring Work Attitudes in the Early Childhood Setting.* 3rd ed. Lake Forest, IL: New Horizons.

Bloom, P.J., A. Hentschel, & J. Bella. 2016. *A Great Place to Work: Creating a Healthy Organizational Climate.* 2nd ed. Lake Forest, IL: New Horizons.

Bodrova, E., & D.J. Leong. 2018. "Common Assessment Terms and How to Use Them: A Glossary for Early Childhood Educators." In *Spotlight on Young Children: Observation and Assessment,* eds. H. Bohart & R. Procopio, 15–20. Washington, DC: NAEYC.

BrightHR & Robertson Cooper Ltd. 2015. *It Pays to Play.* Report of BrightHR & Robertson Cooper Ltd. Manchester, UK: BrightHR & Robertson Cooper Ltd.

Bronfenbrenner, U. 1988. "Interacting Systems in Human Development, Research Paradigms: Present and Future." In *Persons in Context: Developmental Processes,* eds. N. Bolger, A. Caspi, G. Downey, & M. Moorehouse, 25–49. New York: Cambridge University Press.

Bustamante, A.S., K. Hirsh-Pasek, & R.M. Golinkoff. 2017. "The Premature Death of the Whole-Child Approach in Preschool." *Education Plus Development* (blog), June 8. www.brookings.edu/blog/education-plus-development/2017/06/08/the-premature-death-of-the-whole-child-approach-in-preschool.

Camilli, G., S. Vargas, S. Ryan, & W.S. Barnett. 2010. "Meta-Analysis of the Effects of Early Education Interventions on Cognitive and Social Development." *Teachers College Record* 110 (3): 579–620.

Carter, M., & D. Curtis. 2010. *The Visionary Director: A Handbook for Dreaming, Organizing, and Improvising in Your Center.* 2nd ed. St. Paul, MN: Redleaf Press.

Child Welfare Information Gateway. 2016. *Mandatory Reporters of Child Abuse and Neglect.* Washington, DC: US Department of Health and Human Services, Children's Bureau. www.childwelfare.gov/pubPDFs/manda.pdf.

Derman-Sparks, L., D. LeeKeenan, & J. Nimmo. 2015. *Leading Anti-Bias Early Childhood Programs: A Guide for Change*. New York: Teachers College Press; Washington, DC: NAEYC.

Dodge, D.T. 2004. "Early Childhood Curriculum Models: Why, What and How Programs Use Them." *Child Care Information Exchange* 155 (January/February): 71–75. https://ccie-catalog .s3.amazonaws.com/library/5015571.pdf.

Epstein, A.S. 2014. *The Intentional Teacher: Choosing the Best Strategies for Young Children's Learning*. Rev. ed. Washington, DC: NAEYC; Ypsilanti, MI: HighScope Press.

Epstein, A.S., L.J. Schweinhart, A. DeBruin-Parecki, & K.B. Robin. 2004. "Preschool Assessment: A Guide to Developing a Balanced Approach." *Preschool Policy Matters*. Issue 7. New Brunswick, NJ: National Institute for Early Education Research; Ypsilanti, MI: HighScope Educational Research Foundation. http://nieer.org/wp-content/uploads/2016/08/7-1.pdf.

Epstein, J.L., M.G. Sanders, S.B. Sheldon, B.S. Simon, K.C. Salinas, N.R. Jansorn, F.L. Van Voorhis, C.S. Martin, B.G. Thomas, M.D. Greenfeld, D.J. Hutchins, & K.J. Williams. Forthcoming. *School, Family, and Community Partnerships: Your Handbook for Action*. 4th ed. Thousand Oaks, CA: Corwin.

Espinosa, L.M. 1997. "Personal Dimensions of Leadership." In *Leadership in Early Care and Education,* eds. S.L. Kagan & B.T. Bowman, 97–104. Washington, DC: NAEYC.

Forester, J. 2013. *Planning in the Face of Conflict: The Surprising Possibilities of Facilitative Leadership*. Chicago: Planners Press.

Forman, G., & B. Fyfe. 2012. "Negotiated Learning Through Design, Documentation, and Discourse." In *The Hundred Languages of Children: The Reggio Experience in Transformation,* 3rd ed., eds. C. Edwards, L. Gandini, & G. Forman, 247–271. Santa Barbara, CA: Praeger.

Frede, E., & D.J. Ackerman. 2007. "Preschool Curriculum Decision-Making: Dimensions to Consider." *Preschool Policy Brief*. Issue 12. New Brunswick, NJ: National Institute for Early Education Research. www.isbe.net/documents/preschool_curriculum.pdf.

Freire, P. 1970. *Pedagogy of the Oppressed*. Trans. M.B. Ramos. New York: Herder and Herder.

Freire, P. 1985. "Reading the World and Reading the Word: An Interview with Paulo Freire." *Language Arts* 62 (1): 15–21.

Gerber, E.B., M. Whitebrook, & R.S. Weinstein. 2007. "At the Heart of Child Care: Predictors of Teacher Sensitivity in Center-Based Child Care." *Early Childhood Research Quarterly* 22 (3): 327–46.

Gould, E. 2015. "Child Care Workers Aren't Paid Enough to Make Ends Meet." *Economic Policy Institute Issue Brief*. Issue 405. Washington, DC: Economic Policy Institute. www.epi.org /files/2015/child-care-workers-final.pdf.

Hassinger-Das, B., K. Hirsh-Pasek, & R.M. Golinkoff. 2017. "The Case of Brain Science and Guided Play: A Developing Story." *Young Children* 72 (2): 45–50.

Helm, J.H., & L.G. Katz. 2016. *Young Investigators: The Project Approach in the Early Years*. 3rd ed. New York: Teachers College Press.

HHS (US Department of Health and Human Services) & ED (US Department of Education). 2016. "Policy Statement on Expulsion and Suspension Policies in Early Childhood Setting." Joint policy statement. Washington, DC: HHS & ED. www2.ed.gov/policy/gen/guid/school-discipline/policy -statement-ece-expulsions-suspensions.pdf.

Hill, L., & K. Lineback. 2011. *Being the Boss: The 3 Imperatives for Becoming a Great Leader*. Boston: Harvard Business Review Press.

Howell, J., & K. Reinhard. 2015. *Rituals and Traditions: Fostering a Sense of Community in Preschool.* Washington, DC: NAEYC.

Jordan, B., Y.-P. Tseng, N. Coombs, A. Kennedy, & J. Borland. 2014. "Improving Lifetime Trajectories for Vulnerable Young Children and Families Living with Significant Stress and Social Disadvantage: The Early Years Education Program Randomised Controlled Trial." *BMC Public Health* 14 (965): e1–e10. doi:10.1186/1471-2458-14-965.

Katz, L.G., S.C. Chard, & Y. Kogan. 2014. *Engaging Children's Minds: The Project Approach.* 3rd ed. Santa Barbara, CA.: Praeger.

Krechevsky, M., B. Mardell, M. Rivard, & D. Wilson. 2013. *Visible Learners: Promoting Reggio-Inspired Approaches in All Schools.* San Francisco: Jossey-Bass.

Mardell, B., D. Wilson, J. Ryan, K. Ertel, M. Krechevsky, & M. Baker. 2016. "Towards a Pedagogy of Play." Working paper. Cambridge, MA: Project Zero, Harvard Graduate School of Education. www.pz.harvard.edu/sites/default/files/Towards%20a%20Pedagogy%20of%20Play.pdf.

McDonald, D. 2009. *Elevating the Field: Using NAEYC Early Childhood Program Accreditation to Support and Reach Higher Quality in Early Childhood Programs.* Public policy report of NAEYC. Washington, DC: NAEYC. www.naeyc.org/sites/default/files/globally-shared/downloads/PDFs/our-work/public-policy-advocacy/NAEYCpubpolReport.pdf.

Moll, L.C., C. Amanti, D. Neff, & N. Gonzales. 1992. "Funds of Knowledge for Teaching: Using a Qualitative Approach to Connect Homes and Classrooms." *Theory Into Practice* 31 (2): 132–41.

NAEYC. 2009. "Where We Stand on Responding to Linguistic and Cultural Diversity." Position statement supplement. Washington, DC: NAEYC. www.naeyc.org/sites/default/files/globally-shared/downloads/PDFs/resources/position-statements/diversity%20%281%29.pdf.

NAEYC. 2016. *Code of Ethical Conduct and Statement of Commitment.* Brochure. Rev. ed. Washington, DC: NAEYC.

NAEYC. 2017. "Streamlined Model Candidacy Materials." www.naeyc.org/sites/default/files/globally-shared/downloads/PDFs/accreditation/early-learning/Streamlined%20Candidacy%20Materials%20-%20September%202017%28RE%29_0.pdf.

NAEYC. 2018. "Power to the Profession Overview." Accessed March 27. www.naeyc.org/our-work/initiatives/profession/overview.

National Center on Child Care Quality Improvement. 2015. "Overview of the QRIS Resource Guide." Administration for Children and Families, Office of Child Care. https://qrisguide.acf.hhs.gov/files/QRIS_Resource_Guide_2015.pdf.

NCECQA (National Center on Early Childhood Quality Assurance). 2017. "Early Learning and Developmental Guidelines." https://childcareta.acf.hhs.gov/sites/default/files/public/075_1707_state_elgs_web_final.pdf.

NCECQA (National Center on Early Childhood Quality Assurance). 2018. "About QRIS." *QRIS Resource Guide.* Accessed March 20. https://qrisguide.acf.hhs.gov/index.cfm?do=qrisabout.

Neugebauer, R. 2008. "Preparing and Using Monthly Financial Reports." In *The Art of Leadership: Managing Early Childhood Organizations*, rev. ed., eds. B. Neugebauer & R. Neugebauer, 129–131. Redmond, WA: Exchange Press.

NRC (National Research Council). 2000. *Eager to Learn: Educating Our Preschoolers.* Washington, DC: National Academies Press. doi:10.17226/9745.

NYCECPDI (New York City Early Childhood Professional Development Institute). 2009. "Improving the Quality of Early Childhood Education Through System Building." Policy brief, Vol. 2, No. 1. New York: New York City Early Childhood Professional Development Institute. www.earlychildhoodnyc.org/pdfs/Policy%20Brief%202_1.pdf.

O'Neill, C., & M. Brinkerhoff. 2018. *Five Elements of Collective Leadership for Early Childhood Professionals*. St. Paul, MN: Redleaf Press; Washington, DC: NAEYC.

Powell, D.R. 1998. "Reweaving Parents into the Fabric of Early Childhood Programs." *Young Children* 53 (5): 60–67.

Power, T.G. 2000. *Play and Exploration in Children and Animals*. Mahwah, NJ: Lawrence Erlbaum Associates.

QRIS NLN (QRIS National Learning Network). 2017. "QRIS State Contacts and Map." Last modified January 15. www.qrisnetwork.org/qris-state-contacts-map.

Riley-Ayers, S. 2018. "Introduction." In *Spotlight on Young Children: Observation and Assessment,* eds. H. Bohart & R. Procopio, 1–5. Washington, DC: NAEYC.

Rogoff, B. 2003. *The Cultural Nature of Human Development*. New York: Oxford University Press.

Schmidt, C.A. 2017. *The Child Care Director's Complete Guide: What You Need to Manage and Lead*. St. Paul, MN: Redleaf Press.

Schön, D.A. 1983. *The Reflective Practitioner: How Professionals Think in Action*. New York: Basic Books.

Schwarz, R.L., S.M. MacDermid, R. Swan, N.M. Robbins, & C. Mathers. 2003. *Staffing Your Child Care Center: A Theoretical and Practical Approach*. Report of the Military Family Research Institute at Purdue University (MFRI). West Lafayette, IN: MFRI.

Talan, T.N., & P.J. Bloom. 2011. *Program Administration Scale: Measuring Early Childhood Leadership and Management*. 2nd ed. New York: Teachers College Press.

Turner, D., & T. Greco. 2001. *The Personality Compass: A New Way to Understand People*. London: Thorsons.

Venables, D.R. 2015. "The Case for Protocols." *Educational Leadership* 72 (7). www.ascd.org /publications/educational-leadership/apr15/vol72/num07/The-Case-for-Protocols.aspx.

Weisberg, D.S., K. Hirsh-Pasek, R.M. Golinkoff, A.K. Kittredge, & D. Klahr. 2016. "Guided Play: Principles and Practices." *Current Directions in Psychological Science* 25 (3): 177–182.

Yoshikawa, H., C. Weiland, J. Brooks-Gunn, M.R. Burchinal, L.M. Espinosa, W.T. Gormley, J. Ludwig, K.A. Magnuson, D. Phillips, & M.J. Zaslow. 2013. "Investing in Our Future: The Evidence Base on Preschool Education." Research brief. Washington, DC: Society for Research in Child Development. www.fcd-us.org/assets/2016/04/Evidence-Base-on-Preschool-Education-FINAL .pdf.

Acknowledgments

Writing a book is like creating a dance. You can choreograph the moves, but what the dancers bring to the performance makes all the difference. We would like to acknowledge all the support and input we received that helped us create the dance.

This book would not be possible without the many program directors across the country who we've met over the past three years at national conferences, during site visits, and through formal interviews. They informed our thinking and provided anecdotes that helped make our words come alive. Many of the examples and quotes in this book are composites from the voices we heard from directors who work in urban, suburban, and rural areas. We heard from first-year directors and directors who had retired after many years of service. We specifically want to extend our appreciation to the following directors who gave us in-depth interviews: Rudi Andrus, Kimberly Cothran, Sarah Felstiner, Cheryl McNulty, John Nimmo, Polly Smith, Ilene Stark, Brendan Wells, and Lesa Valenzuela.

We thank the attendees of our session, "Facilitated Leadership: How Do Our Skills in Teaching Children Translate into Teaching Teachers?," at NAEYC's 2016 Annual Conference in Los Angeles for sharing their greatest challenges and rewards as early childhood leaders. And of course, our foundation comes from our shared experiences at the Eliot-Pearson Children's School at Tufts University in Medford, MA. We extend our gratitude to our colleagues and friends who worked with us there from 1996 to 2013. Your imprint is part of this too.

A special thank-you to Noelle McCullough, Debbie J. Pischke, and Alyson Williams for their consulting work on select chapters, and to NAEYC staff members Susan Hedges, Tony Durborow, Kristen Johnson, and Cassandra Ryan for their helpful feedback.

Our thanks also go to Kathy Charner, Editor in Chief of NAEYC Books and Related Resources, for her initial invitation at NAEYC's 2015 National Institute for Early Childhood Professional Development in New Orleans to write this book as well as for her encouragement and advice over the past three years. She emphasized the need for a book that is accessible and practical for early childhood education directors with a wide range of experiences. We also thank our editors at NAEYC, Rossella Procopio and Holly Bohart, for their comprehensive help.

Writing a book while working, raising a family, and moving cross-country is not a small feat. We must acknowledge and extend our appreciation and love to our families for all of their support.

This book is dedicated to the leaders of early childhood programs everywhere and to our children and grandchildren.

About the Authors

Debbie LeeKeenan is an early childhood consultant, lecturer, and author. She was director and lecturer at the Eliot-Pearson Children's School, the laboratory school affiliated with the Eliot-Pearson Department of Child Study and Human Development at Tufts University in Medford, MA, from 1996 to 2013. She has also held academic teaching positions at Lesley University in Cambridge, MA, and the University of Massachusetts Amherst. Her work has been published in numerous journals and books, including *Young Children, Theory Into Practice,* and the first edition of *The Hundred Languages of Children: The Reggio Emilia Approach to Early Childhood Education.* Her most recent book, coauthored with Louise Derman-Sparks and John Nimmo, is *Leading Anti-Bias Early Childhood Programs: A Guide for Change.*

Debbie holds a master's degree in education from the University of New Mexico. Her areas of expertise include anti-bias education, teacher preparation, inclusive special education, family engagement, leadership development, professional learning communities, and public school partnerships. Debbie has received a number of awards for her outstanding commitment to young children and the early childhood profession, record of distinguished professional achievement, and work in diversity, including the Tufts University Arts and Sciences Faculty/Staff Multicultural Service Award in 2003; the Tufts Bridge Builder Distinction Award in 2009; and the Abigail Eliot Award in 2015.

Iris Chin Ponte, PhD, is director and classroom teacher at the Henry Frost Children's Program in Belmont, MA. She also currently serves as an adjunct faculty member at Lesley University's Graduate School of Education. Iris previously worked for Sesame Street Research at the Children's Television Workshop (now Sesame Workshop) in New York among many other media and research institutions.

Iris was proudly recognized as an Exchange Emerging Leader in 2015. As a former Fulbright Scholar, she has expertise in cross-cultural issues in education. She has taught and conducted extensive preschool research in the United States, the United Kingdom, Taiwan, China, Japan, and Newfoundland. Iris has received various scholarship and fellowship recognitions from the Children's Defense Fund, the Thomas J. Watson Foundation, CBS, and the American Educational Research Association. She has published in the areas of children and technology, behavior management, children's play, outdoor environmental design, and birth parent reunions and heritage trips for adoptees in China.